The Economic Consequences
of the Atlantic Slave Trade

The Economic Consequences
of the Atlantic Slave Trade

Barbara L. Solow

LEXINGTON BOOKS
Lanham • Boulder • New York • Toronto • Plymouth, UK

Published by Lexington Books
A wholly owned subsidiary of Rowman & Littlefield
4501 Forbes Boulevard, Suite 200, Lanham, Maryland 20706
www.rowman.com

10 Thornbury Road, Plymouth PL6 7PP, United Kingdom

British Library Cataloguing in Publication Information Available

Library of Congress Cataloging-in-Publication Data
Solow, Barbara L. (Barbara Lewis)
  The economic consequences of the Atlantic slave trade / Barbara L. Solow.
    pages cm
  Includes bibliographical references and index.
  ISBN 978-0-7391-9246-7 (cloth : alk. paper) — ISBN 978-0-7391-9247-4 (electronic)
1. Slave trade—Africa—History. 2. Slave trade—America—History. 3. Slave trade—Europe—History. I. Title.
  HT901.S65 2014
  306.3'62—dc23
  978-0-7391-9400-3 (pbk : alk, paper)
                                                                    2014005649

Printed in the United States of America

~

Contents

List of Figures, Tables and Charts

~

Preface

This volume brings together the essays of Barbara Solow. Written over a period of twenty-five years, they are primarily concerned with examining the role of slavery in the historical development of modern capitalism. Eric Williams's pioneering *Capitalism and Slavery* (1944) initially put this problem on the agenda of contemporary scholarship. Williams forcefully argued for the importance of slavery and the slave trade in the development of European capitalism and for the role of industrial capitalism in destroying slavery in the British West Indies. Williams's work has set the terms of subsequent discussion and has been the subject of intense debate since its initial publication. The essays gathered in this volume constitute a sustained contribution to the debates around *Capitalism and Slavery*. Within a historical compass far broader than that of Williams, Solow analyzes the role of slavery in the making of modern capitalism. At the same time, the manner in which she addresses the particular issues raised by the "Williams debate" brings forth the originality and breadth of her contributions to the practice of economic history.

Economic history sits uneasily astride economics and history. As an academic subject, it is more frequently taught in departments of economics than in departments of history. Within the discipline of economics it occupies second-class status. It is pulled in one direction by economic theory's claims to universal validity and in another by history's concern for analysis of the particular. These tensions have been exacerbated during the past several decades. On the one hand, the "New Economic Historians," major protagonists in the Williams debate, have elaborated an approach to economic history that has emphasized rigorous quantification and the application of models based on neoclassical economic theory to historical materials. On the other hand, since the "cultural turn," historians outside the field of economic history, and occasionally within it, have been increasingly concerned with small-scale phenomena, individual agency, contingency, and cultural meaning. Within economic history, the space for interaction and dialogue between economics and history has diminished, as the New Economic History has been drawn closer to economics while problems of large-scale historical change have engaged the interest of fewer historians.

Economic historians have properly emphasized the importance of theory in historical analysis. However, the nature of economic theory and the manner in which it is deployed raise serious questions for the practice of economic history. Economists are above all concerned with the present and with future prognostication. They are interested in time insofar as it affects action and are oriented toward the present or at best the medium term. At the same time, the categories and theoretical claims of economic theory, especially neoclassical theory, are regarded as universally valid. These purposes, claims, and procedures may combine in ways that have unfortunate consequences for historical understanding.

Economic history is too often construed, most notably by proponents of the New Economic History, as the application of a universally valid theory to past data. Historical time is formulated by the crude distinction between past, present, and future events. Past time is distinguished from present and future time merely by being over and done with. Further, substantive elements of historically formed economic practices—environment, social relations of production, institutions of market and state, and the material goods actually produced and distributed amongst social actors—are considered as exogenous variables that remain external to the abstract and general categories of economic theory. The result is an approach based on hypothesis testing and model-building that contributes little to our comprehension of historical processes. Only with difficulty can arguments developed according to this perspective engage in a dialogue with the work of historians.

It is in this context that we may appreciate the originality and value of the essays contained in this book. They are a model for economics, not as a finished theory or a fixed model to be applied to the past, but as a way of thinking. While Solow treats the method of economic inquiry as universal, she regards particular economic theorems as valid in specific historical circumstances. She insists at once on historical contextualization of economic concepts and a historical interpretation of economic change. At the same time, rather than treating substantive aspects of economic practice as exogenous variables, she focuses her attention on historically relevant economic relationships.

In Solow's view, the distinguishing feature of slavery is that labor is a capital asset. It represents a new form of property and wealth holding: a capital investment that could be made to yield more wealth. Slavery introduced an elastic labor supply into the European economy. It represented an improved factor of production. However, Solow does not view slavery as an isolated variable. Rather, she emphasizes the importance of the historical combination of slave labor, sugar, and the plantation system. The plantation system provided the organizational form that made slave labor more productive than free labor, while the demand for sugar proved enormously elastic and provided a remarkable vehicle for the expansion of the market and the accumulation of capital.

From this perspective, the essays in this book reconstruct the making and remaking of the slavery/sugar/plantation complex across a broad temporal and spatial sweep. In them, Solow uses economic concepts and models rigorously and judiciously to illuminate historical processes, while remaining sensitive to changing historical conditions and contexts. Whether carefully tracing the slavery/sugar/plantation complex from the medieval Mediterranean, across the Atlantic, to the nineteenth century Caribbean, or its spread from Barbados to the Leeward Islands to Jamaica in the making of Britain's West Indian sugar empire, she remains sensitive to difference and allows us to identify both long-term continuities and historical particularities. Her coherent explanatory account makes a powerful argument for the centrality of slave labor in the development of capitalism, the integration of the Americas into the international economy, and the creation of the historical conditions for industrialization. Around this analytical core, she develops powerful yet nuanced and subtle arguments that open new perspectives on a broad range of issues. These intelligent and perceptive essays are a model of craftsmanship in a demanding discipline. They will be appreciated by students and scholars alike.

Dale Tomich
Binghamton University

Introduction

This book is a collection of essays on slavery reflecting research conducted over a period of twenty-five years. The main theme is the significance of the institution of slavery in modern economic development. Slavery brought the New World into the international economy. With so much abundant land in the New World, landowners there could not attract a labor force. Immigrants could acquire their own holdings without paying rent. To attract a labor force, labor had to be rendered immobile. The slave/sugar/plantation complex imported from the islands off the coast of Africa was the solution.

Sugar was a crop with economies of scale and low costs of coercion: a single overseer could monitor a hundred slaves planting cane, thus preventing slave resistance and sabotage. Demand for sugar was large and elastic. The industry was organized on efficient capitalist principles. The introduction of slavery gave rise to a large Atlantic trading system joining England, Africa, Brazil and the British West Indies, and England's North American colonies. Regions connected with this system underwent urbanization and economic growth. Regions unconnected languished.

The establishment of the Atlantic trading system turned the English economy in that direction and increased exports, especially manufactured exports. England's colonies in New England, which had hitherto only a trickle of beaver and wood to export, now found a market in the British West Indies, and with the proceeds of these exports became an important customer for English manufacturers. In this way, the institution of slavery was fundamental in bringing the Industrial Revolution to England.

Once the new industrial society was under way, its sources of growth lay not in the protective trade policy that managed the old system but in innovation and technical change. Free trade was the optimal commercial policy. The old British West Indian colonies were declining as other lower-cost producers appeared, and petitioning Parliament for bounties and subsidies, could no longer pretend to be the driving force of English industrial development. That gave the new manufacturing and the Abolitionists an open door to push against in their campaign to abolish the slave trade. They succeeded in 1807.

These ideas did not originate with me. The presiding spirit is that of Eric Williams, whose *Capitalism and Slavery* (University of North Carolina Press, 1944) first pioneered them. That work has been criticized and labeled "controversial," but recent research with better data and more sophisticated analytic methods has come to its support. The "decline" thesis remains under vigorous attack.

The first chapter, "Capitalism and Slavery in the Exceedingly Long Run," traces the transition of the sugar/slave/plantation complex from its origin in Sassanid Mesopotamia, Cyprus, Crete, Andalusia and the islands off Africa, ultimately to Brazil and the British West Indies, to join the New World with the Old. Even before Columbus discovered America, this sugar/slave/plantation economy was conducted on capitalist principles: it amounted to international agribusiness at a time when Western Europe was still in a feudal system.

"Slavery and Colonization," the next chapter, discusses the economic origins of New World slavery. It explains why, when landowners could not attract a labor force, the South and the West Indies chose slavery while the North opted for yeoman agriculture.

The third chapter briefly reviews some criticisms of *Capitalism and Slavery* and shows that important contemporary research confirms Eric Williams's hypothesis that the slave/sugar/plantation complex was a fundamental factor in the onset of the Industrial Revolution in England; that abolition of the slave trade occurred when the older British islands were in decline; and that racism was the consequence, not the cause, of slavery.

The title is self-explanatory in chapter 4, "Why Columbus Failed: The New World Without Slavery." The next chapter, "Caribbean Slavery and British Growth" discusses how slavery was fundamental to the beginning of England's Industrial Revolution. Chapter 6, "Marx, Slavery, and American Economic Growth," draws an analogy between slavery and the enclosure movement in England in providing capital for industrialization, with the common factor being the establishment of private property rights when none had existed previously.

Finally, "The Transition to Plantation Slavery: The Case of the British West Indies," examines the spread of slavery from Barbados to the Leeward Islands and to Jamaica in terms of demand for the product and varying cost conditions in the islands.

These papers were assembled, edited, and prepared for publication by Heidi Feldman, Dan Duling, and my daughter Katherine Solow as a labor of love when I was unable to do the work myself. I cannot find words to thank them.

—Barbara L. Solow, 2013

CHAPTER ONE

~

Capitalism and Slavery
in the Exceedingly Long Run

In the Mediterranean, Europe had developed on a large scale the sugar in-dustry learned from India and the Middle East. Important centres of produc-tion were Sicily and Cyprus, and the large plantation and large factory had evolved. . . . European experience with colonial labor [had evolved] based firstly on the Moorish domination of Spain and secondly on the Portuguese conquest of West Africa. . . . When Columbus set out for the New World, his equipment included the European wanderlust, a powerful economic impulse, the requisite technical aids, a dominant crusading motive, all backed by the necessary political organization. Above all he took with him the knowledge that Africa was a capacious reservoir of labor which could become (as Gil-berto Freyre of Brazil has described the Negro) "the white man's greatest and most plastic collaborator in the task of agrarian colonization."[1]

European expansion did not begin with Columbus, and the economic organization of the Atlantic economy is not of northern European origin. European expansion started at the end of the eleventh century when Chris-tians from southern and Western Europe conquered and exploited economi-cally the lands of Muslim Palestine. The wave of expansion moved from east to west, terminating in the New World; in form and content it was one continuous movement. Atlantic colonization cannot be understood without considering the late medieval colonies of the Mediterranean, the Atlantic archipelagoes, and a large part of Africa, as well as the American continent and the countries of northern Europe. The network of trade routes and of the international balance of payments joined Era with England, Madeira with

Boston, Newfoundland with the Mediterranean, Holland with the West Indies, and Africa with northern Europe. The crucial importance of slavery to the development of the modern world will be missed by narrow nationalistic approaches.

Early Italian Colonization in the Mediterranean
The Mediterranean phase of expansion was not confined to trade and commerce: the Italians, from the time of the First Crusade, engaged in colonial export-oriented sugar production. This production was not feudal: it was not based on a half-free caste of serfs owing labor dues, but involved plantation slavery from the beginning. To a large extent, it was via this first colonial sugar production that the medieval economy of the Mediterranean passed to the modern colonial economy of the Atlantic, and the history of sugar production is the history of slavery. Although Verlinden was concerned to show that it was the Italians who, "under a foreign flag, contributed powerfully to the realization and securing of the passage of civilization from the Mediterranean to the Atlantic world," it was the slaves who, through their labor, provided the principal economic vehicle of this passage. The slave/sugar complex was the bridge over which European civilization crossed from the Old World to the New, not the only bridge, but the first and for three centuries the most important and enduring: it organized the Atlantic economy and dominated it until the nineteenth century.[2]

From its origin in the South Pacific, sugar spread to Southeast Asia and India and was brought to the West by the Arabs in the Muslim era. In the late Sassanid period the southeastern region of Mesopotamia (Khuzistan) was the most important sugar-producing region, and sugar spread with Islam, appearing next in Egypt. From the Muslim era, sugar and slavery were associated.[3]

It is not the volume of the sugar trade but its precedent as an economic organization that is significant. The Italians had sugar plantations among other forms of colonial exploitation; slaves worked these plantations among other occupations; and non-slave workers as well as slaves produced sugar in the Muslim areas. From these beginnings, however, there emerged a definite institution—the sugar plantation with slave labor producing for an export market—that would be transported westward in its developed state. By the fifteenth century, sugar plantations increasingly became not one form but *the* form of colonial exploitation in the Atlantic, and work on these plantations became not one occupation of slaves but *the* occupation, and slaves became not *one* form of labor for sugar production but *the* form. It is clear that slavery had an economic not merely a racial explanation. Plantation slaves were not all black at first, and black slaves were not plantation slaves at first—the black slaves of the Middle Ages were primarily in domestic service—but when colonization moved to the Atlantic, plantation slavery became black and blacks became plantation slaves. But there is a continuum from medieval slavery in Europe to Italian slavery in the Levant to colonial slavery in the Atlantic.

Europeans lost little time commercially exploiting the commodity they discovered during the First Crusade, and the Italian colonies in the Levant became the provider of sugar to all of Christian Europe. After the capture of Tyre from the Fatimids in 1123, Venice proceeded to engage in the sugar industry that it found in its new possessions. After the Fourth Crusade Venice acquired new territories, including Crete, where it expanded the existing sugar industry. After the last Christian fortresses fell and the Europeans withdrew to Cyprus, that island became Europe's principal sugar supplier. Both Venice and Genoa were extensively involved in the slave trade on Crete and Cyprus, and both utilized slaves in production.[4]

Although in Western Europe, by the tenth century, slavery had been succeeded by serfdom practically everywhere, along the shores of the Mediterranean it remained widespread. Until the fifteenth century the Mediterranean world used slaves in a variety of ways: as domestic servants, as soldiers, and in mining and agricultural production. But the last would be the slave institution of the future: European colonization was associated with sugar; sugar was associated with slavery; and slavery was associated with blacks. The richest colonies were those that grew sugar with black slaves, and black slaves in greater numbers appeared in colonies which grew sugar. The slave/sugar complex which originated in the Italian colonies of the eastern Mediterranean shared with gold and silver the honors for first developing the New World and was the more important of the two. An even stronger statement can be made: the slave/sugar complex shared with spices and precious metals the honors for developing economic relations with the entire Third World and was the most important of the three.

Crete became the most important Venetian colony in the Levant, more valuable than the Holy Land colonies. From their occupation in the thirteenth century, the Venetians conducted an important slave market on Crete and cultivated the rural areas with the labor of Greek serfs and slaves. We know from a document of 1393, that Venice subsidized the purchase of slaves in order to develop unoccupied lands in the interior of the island. Furtado calls Brazil "the first large-scale colonial and agricultural enterprise in the Western Hemisphere," but Brazil was merely one stepping stone in a progression that began in the Italian colonies of the Mediterranean.[5]

Although Cyprus was acquainted with sugar from the Arab occupation of the seventh century, sugar's importance there dates from the collapse of the Christian kingdoms in the Holy Land. Along the south shore the royal family maintained plantations and used the sugar for debt repayment. The Hospitalers, the Bishop of Limassol, and the Catalan family of Ferrer all had sugar plantations on Cyprus, but most of our information comes from the holdings of the Cornaro family of Venice. Their methods were fully capitalistic. The plantations were worked by emigrants from the Holy Land, local serfs, and slaves of Arab and Syrian origin. Hydraulic mills were used to process the cane, and disputes over water rights were recorded. Capital equipment, in the form of huge copper boilers, was imported from Italy. The Cornaros even refined their own sugar and exported loaves and powdered sugar. It is clear that large investments and a complex economic organization were required for the entire undertaking.

Thus, while the agriculture of Western Europe was still characterized by manorial society—with serfs providing for their own consumption and meeting a traditionally set level of charges to lord, state, and church; generating most of their own inputs from their own holdings; and being hedged in by communal limitations on decision-making and by a tenurial system that was a web of customary rights and obligations—the members of the Cornaro family were involved in an international agri-business. Their aim was to maximize profits by combining inputs of labor and capital from different places, processing output, and selling the product through a distant marketing network. All of Europe was supplied with sugar from these Italian colonies, together with contributions from Sicily, Muslim Spain, and the Algarve. Slavery plays a role in the development of capitalist forms of economic organization from their first appearance.[6]

Slavery and Colonialism

The slave/sugar complex became the premier institution of European expansion for reasons that are easy to understand. First, the effect of slavery as an economic institution was like abolishing child labor laws or factory acts which limited hours of work: an increased supply of labor was introduced into the economy. And to the extent that the supply of slave labor was more elastically supplied, it increased overall elasticity. Second, if slave labor were more productive than free labor—for example, if it were associated with economies of scale, as Fogel and Engerman maintain—then the introduction of slavery also resembled the invention of a new, improved factor of production, like a new kind of machine. Finally, in permitting slavery, society invented a new form of holding wealth: slave labor could be held as an asset in the portfolio of the saver. It brought this productive factor into the category of capital, since slave labor was purchased outright and delivered a stream of services in future periods. Without slavery, labor could never be a capital asset because free labor could only be rented.[7]

The importance of the institution of slavery in unoccupied or under-populated places like the Atlantic islands and the New World was great. (It had been foreshadowed in the case of the interior of Crete.) What ways were open to Europeans for the exploitation of newly conquered lands? If a flourishing economy existed, the conqueror could loot it, could engage in legitimate trade, or could introduce elements of coercion into the trade to his own advantage. Thus, the Spanish looted the gold of Peru when they ripped it off the walls; the Portuguese forced the trade of India into certain channels and levied exactions on it; and the Dutch forced deliveries in kind in their far eastern possessions. If there had been no economic activity in the colony, these avenues would not have been open. The Europeans could have sent settlers, but there would have been nothing to attract investment from Europe.

As Domar has shown, under some plausible assumptions, of the three elements of a simple agricultural structure—free land, free labor, and a landowning aristocracy—any two elements can exist but not all three simul-taneously. Where land is free, its ownership receives no return. There is no way for Europeans at home to benefit by investing in land or capital in the simplest agricultural situation, and the empty colony will be characterized by family farms whose modest capital needs will be supplied by their own sav-ings. The development of such an economy depends on population growth and domestic capital accumulation. Growth may be vast in the long run but it will be slow to develop.[8]

But if society invents or adopts a productive asset (like slaves) in which capital can be immediately invested, the colony can be built up without waiting for population voluntarily to immigrate or capital to be generated. The factors of production can be assembled at once, and the return to the European investor can be transferred by the export of colonial produce. The existence of the slave institution could have increased the incentive to save in Europe; it is even likelier that it would have switched existing savings to more productive uses. If the alternative uses for savings had been wars, ca-thedrals, and luxury consumption, the adoption of slavery could have been important. If the demand for investment had hitherto been a restraint on growth, the invention of slavery as a productive asset could have played a role. Potentially then, slavery, by introducing an elastic supply of an espe-cially productive sort to the economy, by possibly increasing savings rates, and by enabling savings to be invested more productively, resulted in greater European income and more trade, with all the benefits that division of labor and gains from trade provided. To the extent that colonial slave production was in agriculture, Europe's comparative advantage shifted to manufactures. Had the slaves been engaged in the production of transistors, European agriculture would have been encouraged.[9]

It is neither necessary nor sufficient that this scenario lead to an industrial revolution. The outcome remains to be seen in the historical record. The historical story is that the Italians transferred the sugar/slave complex, which they had developed as a means of colonial exploitation, to Madeira, the Canaries, and the West African islands. The consequent flows of capital, labor, sugar, and manufactures turned these colonies one by one into centers of international trade, uniting them with Europe and Africa in a complex web of transactions. Slavery opened investment opportunities for Europe and allowed northern Europe to trade its manufactures for sugar. I argue that the spread of the slave/sugar complex played a major role in the discovery and economic exploitation of America, as first the Dutch and then the English and French transferred these institutions to Brazil and the Caribbean. This microcosm of capital and trade flows associated with plantation slavery became quantitatively important for British economic development in the eighteenth century. But the *mechanism* which accomplished this development existed in miniature all along the route from Palestine to Crete to Madeira to the Canaries to Sao Tome to Brazil and to the Caribbean.

Transfer of the Sugar/Slave Complex to the Atlantic

Already known to the Genoese in the fourteenth century, Madeira was rediscovered in 1425, by two Portuguese in the service of Prince Henry the Navigator. The islands were entirely uninhabited. The Portuguese exploited their discovery by introducing the slave/sugar complex.

When the Turkish conquest reduced Europe's sugar supply from the eastern Mediterranean, parts of Spain, Portugal, and Italy became alternative sources. Of these, Sicily was the most important. The Sicilian sugar industry had been in trouble at various times, and when it finally declined the Genoese introduced sugar cane production to Madeira. Before the middle of the century (1443), the importation of African slaves began. It was black slavery that was chiefly used in Madeiran sugar production. By 1456, sugar was being exported to England and later to Flanders.

Madeiran cultivation was so successful, and the production so plentiful, that the price of sugar on European markets probably fell by about fifty per cent between the years 1470 and 1500. . . . Madeira, by the time Columbus sailed to the Americas, had become well integrated into the economies of Europe and Africa. The island was the prototype of that momentous and tragic social and economic system of sugar and slavery that was to be repeated, on a far larger scale, in the West Indies and Brazil. By 1500, when Madeira had reached only its seventy-fifth year of settlement, the island had become the world's largest producer of sugar and, with its complex European and African connections, was also an important center for commercial shipping and navigation. . . . The development of the virgin territory of Madeira was, one may say, quite rapid; within two generations the colonists had seized upon their indispensable cash crop and promoted it with astounding success.[10] Duncan should have added that the colonists had also seized upon their indispensable labor supply.

Compare the quotation above with Furtado's description of sugar production in Brazil. And we meet it again in Barbados: "Few enterprises in the history of agriculture in modern times approach this in ingenuity, completeness, and ultimate consequences." The historians of Madeira, of Brazil, and of Barbados, independently of one another, are describing in similar words the same phenomenon. Historians of slavery would recognize the identity of the three cases: in each case slavery is critical. So distinguished an authority on the Atlantic as Chaunu, however, missed the role of slavery. Chaunu emphasizes that the first long phase of European growth "was rooted in the Atlantic adventure and secondly in the Oriental one"; that "it was the dynamism of sugar interests that led to the exploitation of the Atlantic islands"; and that "sugar was the raison d'être of the original settler populations in the Canaries and Madeira." But he misses the significance of slavery by explaining that sugar came to the islands because "sugar requires a rich soil and a readily available labor force. The islands had these." Madeira had no labor force at all, and the Canaries had to import one. What had to be readily available was slave labor for import.[11]

The first deed for sugar production on Madeira was a contract from Prince Henry: "the contract had no trace of feudal or demesnial form. . . . It started a sort of partnership between the Infante and his squire for the production of sugar." Thus, to an uninhabited island, when it was profitable to do so because of demand and cost conditions in the world market, sugar was introduced, slave labor and capital for plant and equipment were imported, the product was processed and exported to the European market, and the island was integrated into an international economy involving several continents in a thoroughly capitalistic network. A brief period of dominance in sugar ended when new cost and demand conditions emerged, and the pattern was repeated elsewhere. Newly discovered islands without the potential for sugar, like the Azores, were characterized by lagging, hesitant, and intermittent growth and were less important members of the world economy.[12]

Madeiran production began to decline after 1570, as Brazilian sugar undercut it in price. Duncan puts production at forty-five thousand arrobas (an arroba was about twenty-five pounds) in 1600, compared with the maximum of On hundred and fifty thousand. By the beginning of the seventeenth century wine had replaced sugar as Madeira's chief export. But the sugar/slave plantations were not a stepping-stone to the new Atlantic economy in the restricted sense that their importance ended when the next step was taken. On the contrary, when sugar moved on, Madeira remained an important link in the development of Atlantic commerce.[13]

As sugar moved to the Western Hemisphere, first Brazil, then the Caribbean and North America became the most important customers for the wines of Madeira. The wine trade of Madeira was in English hands. English merchants acquired wine by selling English textiles and manufactures, salt fish, and Azorean wheat. The Devonshire towns of Topsham and Barnstaple were large suppliers to Madeira, as was Colchester. The wine ships went either directly to the West Indies or stopped first at Cape Verdes for salt. With the West Indian cargoes of sugar, rum, and molasses, they went directly to England or to New England where they traded for codfish, lumber, and pipe staves. The extent of the market for Madeiran wines depended then on the slave-produced commodities of the Americas, and, although insignificant in quantity, so did the textile trade of some Devon and Suffolk towns. The network of eighteenth-century trade was already in existence, in miniature.

The colonization of the Canary Islands followed that of Madeira, although they had been discovered about 1336 by Lazarotto Malocello, a Genoese in the service of Portugal. The islands were conquered by Castile in the mid-fifteenth century. They were originally occupied by the Guanches, whose simple culture was not unlike that of the Arawak of the West Indies. At an early stage of European occupation the Guanches were enslaved, either for domestic use or export; they also fell prey to plague and obscure sicknesses, much like the indigenous peoples of the New World. They were no bar to Spanish conquest. The earliest European settlers were Portuguese, possibly from Madeira, who farmed small holdings of wheat. When European demand for sugar increased in the fifteenth century, its production spread to those parts of the Canaries where it could be grown. The Canaries became sugar producers because that was the way the Spanish could exploit them economically.[14]

From the beginning, sugar production was carried on by foreign capital. Genoese, Portuguese, and the German banking family of Welzer were sources of the considerable requirements. Portuguese from Madeira probably contributed technical skill in sugar-making. The industry grew rapidly from the establishment of the first mill (1484), until, in the early sixteenth century, production was estimated at seventy thousand arrobas, equal to Madeira's at the time but below its peak. Sugar never completely dominated the Canaries; it would only grow in certain areas. Foreigners with large holdings grew sugar on irrigable land, whereas small settlers, usually Portuguese, raised wheat and wine on rain-fed acreage. Conflict between them was sharp, but efforts to limit foreigners' holdings were nullified by Crown exemption. For example, the Welzers were granted such an exemption, not surprisingly since they were in partnership with the royal secretary.[15]

The role of slavery in Canarian sugar production is not clear. Guanches were not used in sugar, although some of those exported to Madeira may have been. In the Canaries the Guanches were domestic slaves. It is known that Christian pirates from the Canaries kidnapped Berbers and enslaved them on sugar plantations and that black slaves were taken from the nearby African mainland and from Portuguese slave markets. Ordinances existed prohibiting the use of imported slaves in the home, so they must have been brought in for sugar. Fernandez-Armesto believes that they were used in refining, with field labor managed by white sharecroppers with white tenants. Verlinden cites a will of 1527, in which a Spanish plantation owner mentions twenty-three male slaves (of whom twenty were black), two female slaves, and skilled free workers. It seems a fair presumption that black slaves were used in the fields. With all respect to Fernandez-Armesto, if black slaves did not work in the fields and were not allowed to be domestics, and we know that black slaves were being imported, where did they all go?[16]

With only partial use of slaves then, the Spanish monarch chose to exploit the Canaries by joining foreign capital to immigrant labor. The combination produced sugar for the European market. Thenceforth the Canaries took their place in the developing Atlantic economy: capital from Italy, labor from Portugal and Africa, sugar to northern Europe, and textiles from London, Bristol, and the Low Countries. By analyzing forty documents relating to the activities of one merchant, Verlinden shows how this bazaar "functioned as a minute nerve-center on the roads of world trade, uniting by land and sea, England and Flanders with Spain and Italy, and, in the Atlantic, Spain with its possessions in the Antilles." By using the known notarial records, Verlinden shows how sugar incorporated a whole web of international transactions. There was an Atlantic economy in existence before the New World began its economic life, and, when Brazil and the West Indies appeared on the scene, they took starring roles in a play already long in progress.[17]

On his first voyage Columbus stopped at the Canary Islands for nearly a month for repairs to the *Pinta's* rudder and a sail change for the *Nina*. In his first notes from America, on October 12, 1492, he compared the Amerindians with the Guanches. He had set out in the hope of founding monopolistic trading posts in the East but this goal was soon abandoned. In his journal he outlined almost at once the two ways in which Spain could exploit his discovery: by the institution of coerced labor in agriculture or by the extraction of precious metals. On December 16, 1492, he wrote:

> I must add that this island (Hispaniola), as well as the others, belongs to Your Highnesses as securely as the kingdom of Castile. It only needs people to come and settle here, and to give orders to the inhabitants who will do whatever is asked of them. . . . The Indians have no weapons and are quite naked. They know nothing about the art of war and are so cowardly that a thousand of them would not stay to face three of our men. . . . they need only to be given orders to be made to work, to sow, or to do anything useful.

Ten days later exploitation by coerced labor had been forgotten. On December 26, in a frenzy to acquire the baubles Columbus's men had brought, the Indians offered in Columbus's words "incredible quantities of gold for almost anything."[18]

Chaunu comments: "the principles of despoiling a traditional society were established." The Spanish, in fact, did base their policy on the extraction of precious metals. But Chaunu draws attention to the astonishing insight of Columbus's first views of October 12: "They bear the mark of genius. After such a trial and amid such anxiety and uncertainty, he could show this lucidity and this unhurried attention." Chaunu attributes Columbus's initial idea to his familiarity with the Portuguese slave trade. (Between 1482 and 1484 Columbus had participated in at least one voyage to the site of the fort at Elmina on the Gold Coast.) Certainly Madeira was where he saw slaves "working and sowing."[19]

The two methods that Columbus described forecast the main direction of Western Hemispheric history for the next three hundred years. The Spanish aim was the extraction of precious metals, and the history of Spanish Latin America, San Domingo (the Dominican Republic), Puerto Rico, Cuba, and Mexico for three centuries reflect this choice. The Portuguese took the other road and introduced plantation slavery; the history of Brazil, the Caribbean islands of France and Britain, the Chesapeake, South Carolina, and Georgia were dominated by that strategy.

Portugal and Spain in the Western Hemisphere

The great achievements of the Portuguese explorers and the brilliant strategy of Affonso de Albuquerque in gaining complete mastery over the Asian sea routes in the sixteenth century should not obscure Portugal's failure to make much of its vast Asian conquests. It was unopposed by other Europeans for the whole century, and at its end it had nothing to show for its pains but Goa, Macao, and Timor. Its eastern trade declined from the beginning of the seventeenth century, and the economic links of its remaining colonies with Europe were of the frailest.

Portugal's policy was to monopolize trade in certain commodities and to force trade into specific ports where it could exact tolls. But the Portuguese also engaged in legitimate trade, acquiring Asian spices with their earnings as merchants and shippers in the traditional trade of Asia. The spices were shipped to Lisbon where the Dutch transshipped them to the rest of Europe. Only Eurocentric vision prevents us from seeing that quantitatively and qualitatively the important Asian trade was between Asians, not between Europe and Asia. Portugal sent few men, few goods, and little capital, and organized little or no productive activity in Asia. Its simple aim was to divert to its own sea routes a small portion of the great Asian trading system that lay at hand. Indeed, three and a half centuries would pass before Europe became the most important trading partner of Asian countries, before Europeans exported capital and organized production in Asia, and before Asia was turned into a food- and raw-materials-producing exporter and an importer of European manufactures. These revolutionary changes date from the second half of the nineteenth century, not from the sixteenth. In that century the transatlantic trade between Spain and Spanish America employed far more shipping and moved far more goods than did the trade from Portugal to India. If we add Portugal's trade with Africa and Brazil, the predominance of the Atlantic becomes even clearer.[20]

Chaunu describes 1441 as something of an *annus mirabilis* in Portuguese exploration: the caravel was built and the first African slave hunt by Europeans took place. In 1444 Prince Henry personally watched his share of a shipment from Guinea being unloaded. The trade between the Senegal and Sierra Leone was managed from the Cape Verde islands. Some of these barren, arid islands (there are ten of significant size) had been discovered between 1456 and 1460. The islands could support little except goats and a small amount of agriculture; three of them had salt deposits. At first they were the site of a complex trade, involving not only slaves but also wax, ivory, hides, and gum from the mainland; manufactures, metal goods, spirits, baubles, and textiles from Europe; Indian cottons and Molucca spices from Asia via Lisbon; and silver from Latin America. This lively trading economy soon waned and by the seventeenth century "slave-holding and slave-trading were the archipelago's raison d'être, [and] the very basis of its existence as a social and economic complex." The islands were an especially horrible en-trepôt: slaves were always the first victims of chronic droughts.[21]

A decade divides the discovery of the Cape Verdes from the mapping out of the great curve of the Gulf of Guinea. In 1471–72, the Grain Coast, the Ivory Coast, and the Gold Coast were discovered. The following year the Slave Coast was reached and then the Niger Delta. On December 21, 1471 São Tomé was discovered, and on New Year's Day Annobon and Príncipe. Fernando Po was probably discovered on the next expedition. The Southern Hemisphere had been reached.

Scarcely more than a generation later, the Malagueta pepper of the Grain Coast proved inferior, the ivory of the Ivory Coast proved exhaustible, and the climate of the Niger Delta proved too unhealthy for Portuguese occupa-tion. The settlers withdrew to São Tomé and Fernando Po. Unable to exploit the islands by the methods that they had used in Asia, they repeated the old pattern. They brought kidnapped Jews from home and black slaves from Africa and set up sugar plantations. São Tomé was producing sugar for export by 1522, and became a major supplier to Europe. "São Tomé became the true economic and political center of Portuguese power north of Angola," and Angola became a tributary, supplying slaves first to São Tomé then to Brazil. Without them Angola was economically insignificant.[22]

Not only did the Asian trade of the Portuguese dwindle, but so too did the African trade of any commodity except slaves. The most enduring legacy of Portuguese exploration was to open up the coast of Africa for slave supplies.

São Tomé's sugar era was short-lived. Estimates of production suggest a rise until perhaps the last quarter of the century and a decline thereafter. There were slave rebellions in 1580, 1595, and 1617, and more or less con-tinuous guerilla resistance. But it was the entry of Brazil into the sugar market in the last quarter of the century that changed São Tomé from a sugar pro-ducer to a slave entrepôt. The great profitability of that business attracted the Dutch, and the worldwide Luso-Dutch wars of the seventeenth century—if we can call Asia, Africa, and Latin America worldwide—in fact began with a Dutch attack on São Tomé and Principe in 1598–99.

Brazil was not planned as a sugar plantation; it became one by the logic of the situation. Portugal hoped for precious metals. Until these turned up it needed an economic foothold to make Brazil a paying proposition and to keep rivals away. Of the ten captaincies created in the original settlement, only three took hold: two where sugar thrived and one where slave-hunting was the settlers' occupation. The crown soon undertook to encourage sugar production as the most likely road to riches until gold was found. Development was slow at first, but by the middle of the sixteenth century the industry was well established; in the last quarter of the century production increased tenfold. From 1575 to 1650, Brazil supplied most of Europe's sugar and imported considerable quantities of manufactured goods and slaves, not only for itself but also (illicitly) for the Spanish colonies in the Caribbean and on the mainland. The main source of these goods—textiles and hardware—was not Portugal but northern Europe.

The planter who claimed that the sugar of Brazil was more profitable than all the pepper, spices, and luxury goods of Asia was right. Between 1575 and 1650, Pernambuco and Bahia produced several million arrobas of sugar, and Brazil's production exceeded that of the Atlantic islands by a factor of twenty. "From mere plundering and mining ventures . . . the Western Hemisphere started to become an integral part of the European reproductive economy, the technology and capital of which were therefore to be guided and invested in such a manner as to create a permanent flow of goods to Europe."[23]

Furtado makes a crude calculation that Brazil had 120 sugar mills at the end of the century at an average value of £15,000 (gold), amounting to investment in plant and equipment of £1.8 million. Valuing twenty thousand slaves at £25 and assuming that 75 percent were engaged in sugar adds £375,000, for a total investment of £2.175 million. Income can be no more than "a vague conjecture." Furtado estimates sugar exports in a good year at £2.2 million, of which 60 percent is ascribed to value added in Brazil, and of this 75 percent is ascribed to the sugar sector. The resulting income estimate of £2 million to be divided among the three hundred thousand whites of Brazil "was evidently far higher than that prevailing in Europe at the time, and at no other period of its history—even at the height of the gold cycle—did Brazil regain this level of income."[24]

The formidable difficulties of erecting an agricultural export industry of this size in the virgin territory of the Western Hemisphere in the sixteenth century were overcome because the required institutions had already been developed, and Brazil took over from São Tomé the pattern that had been bequeathed from the Italian Mediterranean colonization. But the Dutch now played the role of the Italians. From mid-century the Portuguese sugar industry was amalgamated with Dutch and Flemish interests. Dutch capital financed the acquisition of slaves from Africa and the setting up of plantations; the Dutch had perhaps a half to two thirds of the carrying trade between Europe and Brazil; Antwerp and Amsterdam (after the sack of Antwerp) refined the sugar; and the Dutch marketed it.[25]

If the sixteenth were Portugal's imperial century in Asia and Africa, and Portugal's and Spain's in Latin America, the seventeenth century was Holland's. Its war of independence against Spain was waged equally against Portugal during the union of the crowns. According to Boxer's succinct scorecard, Holland played Portugal in Africa and tied, Holland played Portugal in Asia and won, Holland played Portugal in Brazil and lost. In Africa the Dutch originally succeeded in taking not only the slave forts at Elmina, Shama, and Axim, but also Luanda, Benguela, São Tomé, and Annobon. The latter group they could not retain, thus the tie score, but they had gained enough of a foothold to become a dominant force in the slave trade. In Asia, the Dutch reached the East Indies at the end of the sixteenth century. The Portuguese strategic position, based on facing a mainland enemy, was now outflanked. The Dutch could attack the Portuguese strongholds and attack they did. Malacca, Ceylon, Cochin, and the Malabar Coast fell one by one, and the Asian trade was reoriented from the Red Sea, the Persian Gulf, and East Africa to a direct route from Batavia (Jakarta) round the Cape of Good Hope.

Meanwhile, in Brazil, Dutch occupation had begun in 1630. Portugal, with its limited resources, made the choice to give up Asia in favor of Brazil and its complementary ports in Africa. The Dutch were expelled from Brazil, retaining only Surinam, Essequibo (Guyana), and Demerara (Guyana). The Dutch attack on Spanish shipping in the Western Hemisphere also succeeded. As a result of its depredations "official shipping between Seville and the Indies shrank by 1640, to less than 10,000 tons annually" and continued to shrink for the rest of the century. Spain retained its mainland colonies, but its seapower monopoly had been broken, and it could not prevent French and British settlers from occupying the smaller Caribbean islands.[26]

In the short term, Holland secured a dominant role in the slave trade of Africa and the spice trade of Asia, and, although it lost the sugar trade of Brazil, Brazil lost much of it too when production was introduced into the Caribbean islands. But Dutch commercial and shipping resources made the Caribbean for the first half of the seventeenth century "a Dutch lake."

Sugar production never disappeared from Brazil; nor did Brazil disappear from the Atlantic economy. When sugar revenues declined severely at the end of the seventeenth century, Portugal tried to compensate by encouraging manufacturing in Brazil. It adopted a protectionist policy and almost succeeded in ending textile imports altogether. The powerful Portuguese wine interests found that they could sell less to England if England earned less foreign exchange in Portuguese markets. Together the English and these wine interests maneuvered the Methuen Treaty of 1703: English textiles would no longer be embargoed and Portuguese wines would receive preferential treatment in England. Furtado observes that, in view of the conditions in 1703, the treaty probably had no great effect. The low value of the wine exports could hardly be expected to have balanced textile imports; perhaps the treaty would not have survived. But, by the eighteenth century, gold was finally discovered in Brazil, earning perhaps £2.5 million for Portugal at the peak of production in 1760. The Methuen Treaty provided the mechanism for British manufactures to satisfy the large Brazilian demand for goods. The gold went to Britain and Portugal could only skim off some taxes and brokerage.[27]

As the Marquis de Pombal, the great Portuguese statesman, supposedly said, gold meant nothing more than fictitious riches for Portugal: "even Negroes working in the mines had to get their loincloths from the British." What Portugal did get from the transaction was a British guarantee of its national sovereignty and of its possession of Brazil. Without backing it would have been at the mercy of France and Spain.

Brazil, founded on slaves and functioning with slaves until the late nineteenth century, was an important participant in the Atlantic economy in the sugar and gold eras from the late sixteenth century. The combination of empty land, European capital, and African labor led to production on a much larger scale than its earlier incarnations had ever achieved.

Spain's Latin American colonies, however, never played a major role in international trade after the mining era. The Spanish limited their colonial aims to generating a surplus in gold and silver and remitting it annually to the home country. Settlement was made only along an axis connecting the mining properties and the necessary supply and transport routes. Aside from precious metals, no economic links between the mother country and the colonies were encouraged, nor was any intercolonial trade. In pursuit of this policy Spain tried to monopolize and regulate all the trade to the colonies. Consequently, the supply of shipping, capital, slaves, and settlers was severely limited. When the mining industry declined, the vast Spanish empire sank into stagnation and decay. Not until the Spanish colonies were opened to foreign capital at the end of the eighteenth century did the sugar-slave complex take hold in Cuba, replicating on a grand scale the cases I have described.

Caribbean Slavery and British Economic Growth:
The Eric Williams Hypothesis

The Atlantic economy in the eighteenth century found the Spanish colonies moribund, the Portuguese colony pouring out gold, and the French and British established in the Caribbean and on the seaboard of North America.

The earliest Caribbean colonists struggled to survive by growing tobacco, indigo, cocoa, cotton, ginger, and the like on small plots with indentured labor and some slaves. It was a losing battle. Sugar was introduced to Barbados about 1640, and within a decade the large numbers of small holders and white servants were replaced by large plantations and black slaves. Brazilian sugar could no longer compete, and its markets were henceforth limited to southern Europe. The transformation of Barbados to an economy based on slaves and sugar was followed by that of the Leeward Islands, Guadeloupe, and Martinique, and much later and on a larger scale by Jamaica and Saint Domingue (Haiti). Total sugar production in the Western Hemisphere can be estimated roughly at fifty-four thousand tons in 1700; it doubled by 1740; tripled by 1776; and nearly quadrupled by the end of the American Revolution.

"By 1750, the poorest English farm laborer's wife took sugar in her tea." Rum from West Indian molasses catered to the notorious drinking habits of eighteenth-century Britain and supplied the navy. By 1660, the value of sugar imports exceeded that of all other colonial produce combined; by 1774, sugar accounted for 20 percent of the total import bill, far surpassing any other commodity. The British took a third of Europe's consumption in the first half of the century, and the rapid increase after that has been described as "astonishing"; per capita consumption was eight times that of the French. Slave labor produced this sugar. Of the six million slaves taken from Africa in the eighteenth century, the Caribbean imported more than half and Brazil another third.[28]

Once the sugar/slave plantation arrived in the British colonies, the external trade of Britain turned in that direction. At the beginning of the seventeenth century the woolen industry dominated English trade and manufacturing, accounting for four fifths of English foreign trade, mainly with Europe. Trade with the Levant, India, and Indonesia were sources of imports rather than destinations for exports; the East was a notorious sink for bullion. With the appearance of slave-grown tobacco and sugar, British commerce turned to the West, and Britain became the entrepôt for Europe's supply of these goods. By the end of the seventeenth century the reexport of colonial and Asian goods amounted to over a quarter of British exports. But American trade was just beginning and Asia's share was declining. Demand for spices was satiated and inelastic, and European governments began to ban imports of Asian textiles. The share of Oriental trade would not revive until the rise in the popularity of tea well into the next century.

The total production of sugar and much of the production of tobacco, their cheapness, and their elasticity of supply were dependent upon the continuing flow of the productive labor of slaves to the colonies. The eighteenth century saw the full fruition of this trade reorientation. Total trade increased greatly, and the Atlantic was crisscrossed by British ships carrying manufactured goods to Africa, the West Indies, Brazil, Portugal, and British North America. The Atlantic islands were exporting wine, Africa slaves, Brazil gold, and the West Indies sugar and molasses. Some of the British North American colonies were sending rice and tobacco to Britain; others were sending fish, lumber, horses, and flour to the West Indies and were buying British manufactures with the proceeds. Every one of these flows depended on the product of slave labor.

In particular this dependence on slave labor is true of the North American nonslave colonies. Their land was suited to agricultural commodities which could not easily bear the cost of transport to Britain. They could import British manufactures only by shipping their surplus food and raw materials to the slave colonies of the West Indies and earning there the foreign exchange that enabled them, to meet their balance of payments deficits in Britain. Thus, the international trade of the northern colonies depended on slave production as much as did the trade of Virginia and South Carolina. The population of British North America increased tenfold between 1700 and 1774, and was responsible for most of the expansion of British overseas trade during the middle decades of the century.[29]

Wherever the slave/sugar complex went, a network of international trade flows followed: flows of labor, capital, manufactures, sugar, raw materials, shipping, banking, and insurance. The Atlantic network centered on the Caribbean was similar in form to that centered on the eastern Mediterranean in the late Middle Ages and those centered on the Atlantic islands, the African islands, and Brazil in the early modern period. But this eighteenth-century trading network had a vastly greater significance: it was important to the economic growth of Great Britain at the beginning of the Industrial Revolution. Slavery did not cause the Industrial Revolution, but played an active role in its pattern and timing.

The slave institution increased economic activity in the Atlantic economy: it did not merely direct economic activity from alternative, equally productive channels. Slavery introduced a more elastic supply of labor into the colonial system, counteracting the diminishing productivity of investment, and permitting a period of constant returns to colonial investment, thus raising the rate of return on investment in the whole colonial system over what it would otherwise have been. To the extent that this new slave labor was more productive than free white labor, the return to investment was multiplied even further. In sum, slavery in the colonies raised the rate of return on investment in the empire—made investment more productive—and thereby increased national output. Capital investment in the colonies, amounting to £37 million in 1773, was large enough to make this a significant force.[30]

At higher levels of national output, the British colonial empire enjoyed an extension of the market and a concomitant division of labor, which encouraged British manufacturing activity in particular. The gains accrued to Britain irrespective of the original level of employment in the home country. But if there was underemployment associated with a Keynesian demand shortfall—as I have suggested—the slave colonies made an additional contribution to economic activity through raising total demand.

How do these mechanisms fit with the concrete historical circumstances of British growth in the eighteenth century? It is now generally agreed that national output grew more slowly than previous estimates suggest, and that the acceleration of investment and of industrial growth was more gradual than earlier scholars believed. Amidst these revisions, however, the one relationship that is confirmed more than ever is the importance of exports to industrial growth. There is a solid connection between slave production in the Americas and British production of industrial goods. "In the last two decades of the eighteenth century (the early rather than the decisive phase of the industrial revolution), almost 60 percent of additional industrial output was exported." Industrial exports led industrial growth, and industrial growth meant structural change and overall growth. American slavery contributed substantially to these exports.[31]

To argue that slavery was important for British economic growth is not to claim that slavery caused the Industrial Revolution. British incomes grew over the eighteenth century when population growth was accompanied by increased agricultural productivity, leaving both a demand for nonagricultural commodities, not only by the rich but also by people of middle income levels, and a supply of labor to produce these goods. This entire process paved the way for the technical change which began late in the century and assumed greater quantitative importance in the first quarter of the nineteenth century. One of the new demands was for sugar; and the demand for sugar, originating in the home economy, was a necessary condition for the Atlantic trading system. But so too was the elastic supply of productive labor to produce that sugar.

The late eighteenth century was an era of radical change for the British economy, and its importance should not be obscured by comparison with future decades. It is hardly surprising that changes in the growth of aggregate output or output per capita show up only with a lag. Industrial growth was marked in the late eighteenth century even though it was smaller than Deane and Cole thought and smaller than it later became. According to Crafts's revised figures, the annual growth rate of industry more than doubled from the period 1700 to 1760 (when it was .71), to the period 1760 to 1780 (1.51), and grew half as much again between 1780 and 1801 (2.11). Aside from government and defense, only one other sector of the eighteenth-century economy grew at a rate exceeding 1 percent over the entire century. All sectoral growth rates exceeded 1 percent after 1801, and industry continued to lead.[32]

Investment grew markedly at the end of the eighteenth century whether one accepts Feinstein's estimates or Crafts's. For Feinstein, gross domestic investment as a percent of gross domestic product rose from 8 percent between 1761 and 1770, to 13 percent between 1791 and 1800, or by 5 percentage points in one generation. For Crafts, the corresponding rise was from 5.7 percent in 1760 to 7.9 percent in 1801, a faster rate of increase than in the period before 1760.[33]

In the late eighteenth century, investment and industrial growth were accelerating and national output began to grow faster. Crafts's table 5 shows output growth rates of .69 for 1700 to 1760, and .70 for 1760 to 1780, but 1.32 for 1780 to 1801. I have argued that some portion of the investment increase is attributable to the slave-based American economy, and that much of the incremental industrial output of the period depends on the export demand associated with that economy.

Crouzet estimates the growth rate of exports between 1781 and 1800 as more than 5 percent and attributes the export spurt of the 1790s to increased demand from American markets. Export growth accounts for nearly 60 percent of additional industrial growth in this period, and industrial growth contributes to the growth of output. Without the demand for exports generated by the slave-grown crops of the Atlantic economy, Britain would have begun the nineteenth century with a much slower-growing industrial base and a slower-growing economy.[34]

Decadal turning points in the late eighteenth century were fragile because of the effect of the American Revolution. But over the century it remained true that the growth of output, of the investment rate, and of industrial production accelerated. The share of exports in national output doubled over the century and was a source of dynamic changes: export growth led industrial growth which led to accelerated growth in national output. There is no reason to dispute Deane and Cole's conclusion that "the existence of exploitable international markets at the end of the eighteenth and beginning of the nineteenth centuries was probably crucial in initiating the process of industrialization and the growth of real incomes which was associated with it." They claim that "it was the American market (including the valuable West Indies) which provided the greatest scope for growth."[35]

The importance of Caribbean slavery to British growth depended on particular circumstances and was confined to a particular historical period. The old colonial system benefited Britain when investment was lagging, technical change was slow, growth in domestic demand for manufactures was less than that in external demand, and when the North American colonies depended on Britain for manufactures and on the West Indies for the foreign exchange with which to buy them. None of these conditions obtained after the Napoleonic Wars (or by the 1820s at the latest).

By 1820, Britain had moved decisively toward industrialization. Investment and technical change picked up; exports mattered less; within the diminished export sector, North America and the West Indies mattered less; and market-widening gave way to market-deepening as a driving force for exports.

British export growth rates declined after 1802, and remained slow until the middle of the nineteenth century. "It is clear that it was only after 1850, that Britain really became an 'export economy.'" Saul confines the term export economy to the period 1870 to 1914. Exports as a percentage of national income (which had doubled over the eighteenth century to a peak of 18 percent in 1801) fell and stagnated thereafter. The leading role of exports in British economic growth did not survive the eighteenth century, whichever measure one chooses. The home market was expanding faster than demand from abroad, and domestic consumption and investment replaced exports as an engine of growth.[36]

Within the diminished export sector, trade moved away from the United States and West Indies. The American market, which had translated more than half of the British West Indian sugar earnings into British exports, lost importance during the wars and never mattered so much again. This timing is necessarily clouded because Britain had control of Europe's access to overseas trade during the wars, so what was developing was not immediately apparent. The American market ceased to depend on imports from Britain, which, as a colony, she had been constrained to take. The United States began to control her own commercial policy, produce her own textiles and manufactures, and meet her foreign exchange needs from the export earnings of the Cotton South.

The share of the United States in British export growth to the end of the War of 1812, was large, but this was a false dawn. "The Americas, though playing a vital role from the 1780s to the end of the French wars, were thereafter far less important." The mean growth rate of British exports to the United States between 1814 and 1846, was -0.6 in current values, indicating an absolute decrease. Cain and Hopkins go so far as to say that "the rise of an export economy based on cotton manufacturing after 1780 was accomplished only by dismembering the old colonial system." One can quibble about the date, and Americans can question the word "dismembering," but the statement is otherwise correct.[37]

In the era of cotton dominance it was India, Australia, and Latin America which were increasingly Britain's customers. Cain and Hopkins calculate that four fifths of the increase in exports from 1816–1820 to 1838–1842, came from outside the old colonial system. Even in the export field it was the cheapening of British goods that led to export growth, as lower prices expanded foreign demand. Export volumes increased while values stayed fairly steady; market-deepening not market-widening dominated at home and abroad in the first half of the nineteenth century, but the main sources of growth were at home.

British resources directed toward the acquisition of slaves in the eighteenth century were very productive: they hastened the development of the New World; the rate of return on investment in the empire was enhanced; and the earnings associated with slave-produced crops enabled Britain's manufacturing sector to expand very much faster than domestic demand permitted. In the first half of the nineteenth century, with higher investment and faster technical change, market widening through exports mattered much less to British growth, and slavery no longer had a starring role. Emancipation meant buying more sugar from Cuba and Brazil rather than from Trinidad and Demerara. The end of slavery would have been costly to Great Britain had it come in the middle of the eighteenth century. When it came toward the middle of the nineteenth, it was a bargain. Until the nineteenth century, wherever sugar and slavery went, a web of international trading flows in capital, merchandise, labor supply, and shipping was woven. Where slavery did not go, less trade flowed between Europe and the rest of the world. Fanciful tales that European growth was due to exploitation of "the periphery" by "the metropolis" do not withstand scholarly examination. The exploitation that really mattered for three hundred years was the exploitation of African slaves.

Notes

1. Eric Williams, *From Columbus to Castro; the History of the Caribbean, 1492–1969* (London, 1970), 16–17. This quotation illustrates Williams's early understanding that Medieval Italy, Portugal, Holland, England, France, Brazil, Africa, and the Caribbean fitted into a historical pattern which linked slavery with capitalist development. The present article is an elaboration on his original vision.

2. Charles Verlinden, *The Beginnings of Modern Colonization: Eleven Essays with an Introduction* (Ithaca, 1970), xix, xx.

3. Michael Lombard, *The Golden Age of Islam* (New York, 1975), 25; Daniel Pipes, *Slave Soldiers of Islam: Genesis of a Military System* (New Haven, 1981), 13. Paula Sanders, Harvard University, has kindly supplied me with important references to the medieval sugar/slave economy of Islam and Italy. See also, William D. Phillips, Jr., *Slavery from Roman Times to the Early Transatlantic Trade* (Minneapolis, 1984), 66–88.

4. Verlinden, *Beginnings*, 18–19.

5. The documents on slavery in Crete are almost entirely unpublished. Verlinden published the principal work, "La Crete debouche et plaque tournate de la traite des esclaves aux XIV et XV siècles," Studi di onore di A. Fanfani (Milan, 1962), III, 593–669. My source on Cyprus is Verlinden, *Beginnings*, 19–20. Celso Furtado, *Economic Growth of Brazil: A Survey from Colonial to Modeca Times* (Berkeley, 1963), 6.

6. Verlinden, *Beginnings*, 20.

7. Robert W. Fogel and Stanley Engerman, *Time on the Cross* (Boston, 1974), 1, 192–94. Furtado, *Economic Growth of Brazil*, 148.

8. Evsey D. Domar, "The Causes of Slavery or Serfdom: A Hypothesis," *Journal of Economic History*, XXX (1970), 18–32.

9. Aside from the example of slavery, Europeans did not engage in the organization of much productive activity in the rest of the world until the nineteenth century. European entrepreneurship and European direct capital investment assume large proportions only in the last quarter of the century.

10. T. Bentley Duncan, *Atlantic Islands: Madeira, the Azores, and the Cape Verdes in Seventeenth-Century Commerce and Navigation* (Chicago, 1972), 10–11; Verlinden, *Beginnings*, 98–112.

11. Carl and Roberta Bridenbaugh, *No Peace Beyond the Line: The English in the Caribbean, 1624–1690* (New York, 1972). Pierre Chaunu (trans. Katharine Bertram), *European Expansion in the Later Middle Ages* (Amsterdam, 1979), 63, 98, 107.

12. Verlinden, *Beginnings* 216, 217.

13. Duncan, *Atlantic Islands*, 31.

14. Felipe Fernandez-Armesto, *The Canary Islands after the Conquest: The Making of a Colonial Society in the Early Sixteenth Century* (Oxford, 1982), 32, 203.

15. Queen Juana to Anton Welter and Company, Valladolid, Jan. 1513; reproduced in ibid., 219. The conflict between the small settlers and the plantation owners has a familiar ring to Americans.

16. Verlinden, *Beginnings*, 113–31, 153.

17. Ibid., 143.

18. Chaunu, *European Expansion*, 164, 190, n.129.

19. Ibid., 162.

20. John H. Parry, "Transport and Trade Routes," *Cambridge Economic History of Europe* (Cambridge, 1967), IV, 199.

21. Chaunu, *European Expansion*, 120; Duncan, *Atlantic Islands*, 230.

22. Antonio H. de Oliveira Marques, *History of Portugal* (New York, 1972), 274.

23. Furtado, *Economic Growth of Brazil*, 5.

24. Ibid., 47. If Furtado were writing today he might revise the statement, but that would not detract from its forcefulness.

25. C. R. Boxer, *The Dutch in Brazil* (Oxford, 1957), 20.

26. De Oliveira Marques, *History of Portugal*, 338; Edwin E. Rich, "Colonial Settlement and its Labour Problems," *Cambridge Economic History*, IV, 204.

27. Furtado, *Economic Growth of Brazil*, 92. England found in the Portuguese-Brazilian economy a fast expanding and nearly unilateral market. Her exports were paid for in gold, which gave the English economy exceptional flexibility in its operations on the European market. She thus found herself for the first time in a position to balance indirectly her trade in construction materials and other raw materials from northern Europe with manufactured products. The English economy thus acquired greater flexibility and a tendency to concentrate on investments in the manufacturing sector as the most indicated for rapid technological evolution. Further, by receiving most of the gold then being produced in the world, English banking houses reinforced their position even mare and Europe's financial center transferred from Amsterdam to London. According to English sources, imports of Brazilian bullion in London were at one time as high as £50,000 a week, permitting a substantial accumulation of reserves without which Britain could hardly have carried on the Napoleonic Wars.

28. Ralph Davis, *Rise of the Atlantic Economies* (Ithaca, 1973), 351. For a full discussion of the rise of sugar consumption in England, see Sidney W. Mintz, *Sweetness and Power: The Place of Sugar in Modern History* (New York, 1985), 74–151; Philip D. Curtin, *The Atlantic Slave Trade: A Census* (Madison, 1969), 216, Table 65.

29. Davis, *Rise of the Atlantic Economies*, 303.

30. Solow, "Caribbean Slavery and British Growth: The Eric Williams Hypothesis," *Journal of Development Economics*, XVII (1985), 99–115.

31. Nicholas F. R. Crafts, "British Economic Growth," *Economic History Review*, XXXVI (1983), 177–99.

32. Ibid., Table 5. Phyllis Deane and William A. Cole, *British Economic Growth 1688–1959: Trends and Structure* (Cambridge, 1967; 2nd ed.).

33. Charles H. Feinstein, "Capital Accumulation and the Industrial Revolution," in Roderick Floud and Donald McCloskey (eds.), *The Economic History of Britain since 1700* (New York, 1981) 1, Table 7-3, 133.

34. Francois Crouzet, "Towards an Export Economy; British Exports during the Industrial Revolution," *Explorations in Economic History*, XVII (1980), 48–93.

35. Deane and Cole, *British Economic Growth*, 312, 34.

36. Crouzet, "Towards an Export Economy," 81; S. Berrick Saul, "The Export Economy, 1870–1914," *Yorkshire Bulletin of Economic and Social Research*, XVII (1965), 5–18.

37. Crouzet, "Towards an Export Economy," 77, 73; P. J. Cain and Anthony G. Hopkins, "The Political Economy of British Expansion Overseas, 1750–1914," *Economic History Review*,XXXIII (1980), 489.

CHAPTER TWO

~

Slavery and Colonization

When the elder Hakluyt published his promotional tract for the North American colonies in 1585, he painted a picture of a thriving trade in colonial products (wood, oil, wine, hops, salt, flax, hemp, pitch, tar, clapboards, wainscot, fish, fur, meat, hides, marble, granite, sugar), exchanging for British goods (woolens, hats, bonnets, knives, fishhooks, copper kettles, beads, looking glasses, and a thousand wrought wares), lowering British unemployment, promoting manufacturing, and providing advantages to church, crown, and national security. This would require the migration of thirty-one different kinds of skilled workers to America.

If Hakluyt saw any difficulties in achieving this happy state of affairs, a propaganda tract was not the place to mention them. Certainly, Adam Smith would have seen none. Two centuries later he wrote, "The colony of a civilized nation which takes possession either of a waste country, or of one so thinly inhabited, that the natives easily give place to the new settlers, advances more rapidly to wealth and greatness than any other society."[1] Yet from the day Hakluyt wrote until almost the middle of the eighteenth century, economic growth and progress were barely discernible in the colonies, and the North Atlantic economy was of negligible importance. It did not develop automatically or in the manner Hakluyt and Smith envisaged.

In the first section, "Slavery Made the Atlantic Trading System," I argue that firm and enduring trade links between Europe and America were not forged without and until the introduction of slavery; that the eras of privateering, chartered companies, and the early staple trades were not preludes to development, but rather unpromising beginnings leading to stagnation; and that colonial development was strongly associated with slavery. Voluntary labor was slow to immigrate; capital was hard to attract or generate; promising export crops were slow to emerge; and when they did, free labor was reluctant to grow them. African slaves provided much of colonial America's labor, attracted a large share of capital investment, accounted for most of the colonial export crops, and (compared with free labor) conferred wealth and income in greater measure on those places and times where slavery was established.

In the second section, "Colonization Where Land Is Abundant," I argue that this pattern of development is not adventitious but is explained by the difficulties inherent in colonizing regions where land is relatively cheap and abundant.[2] Placing colonial history in the context of "free" land has a long history. It provides that conceptual framework for the period whose absence is so often deplored by historians. And, as a conceptual framework, it has substantial advantages over the available alternatives, whether older ones like the Imperial School of Charles M. Andrews or contemporary ones suggested by John M. McCusker and Russell R. Menard, Bernard Bailyn, or Jack P. Greene and J. R. Pole.

Slavery Made the Atlantic Trading System

To those who saw colonial development as the inexorable working of the Divine Hand of Providence or the only slightly less Divine Hand of Comparative Advantage, the early period just represented stages of growth, and the repeated failures of colonizing attempts were attributed to ad hoc circumstances. Seeing development as foreordained, and Elizabethan sea dogs and Roanoke as stages in an inevitable process, begs the question of providing a conceptual framework that seeks systematically to account for the timing and pattern of growth.

The privateering attacks on Spain, launched by the French, English, and Dutch from the early sixteenth century, have been portrayed as the first stage in developing the Atlantic system and as the opening battle in a war for command of the seas in order to exploit the new discoveries of the western hemisphere. This is an exaggerated Atlantic-centric view. It has been shown that such an interpretation, for example, of the Anglo-Spanish wars, pales before Philip II's interest in crushing heresy and rebellion in northern Europe.[3]

Privateering is better understood less as a prelude to colonization than as an alternative to it. Privateering robs Peter to pay Paul: Whatever the Dutch or French or English gained, the Spanish lost. Worse than a zero-sum game, privateering invites retaliation, increases risk, and discourages settlement and economic activity, which depend upon security from international lawlessness. More plausibly, English governmental policy in the Caribbean turned from encouraging privateering to opposing it when settlement began to promise dividends.

With the notable exception of Massachusetts Bay, chartered companies—Dutch, French, English—failed to found settlements in the Americas. To treat these failures as due to "adverse winds," to having settlers "not of the right stuff," "lack of tenacity," "poor leadership," or "lack of supplies," is to miss the essential difficulties of providing men and capital for colonies under the prevailing economic conditions, which persistence and leadership could not easily overcome. The success of the Massachusetts Bay Colony rested on the strength of its noneconomic motives. The "lack of initiative and vitality" explanation of French colonization does not go far to explain the failure in Canada and the success in the French West Indies.

It is hard to accept that English chartered companies fared badly in America for lack of know-how and entrepreneurial skill when they were demonstrably successful in trading to the Baltic, the North Sea, and the Mediterranean. Here, with abundant land, no labor supply, and no export crop, there would be no surplus for the company. Neither governments nor capitalists were willing indefinitely to invest large sums in colonies under these conditions. The history of failed settlements may thus be more instructive than the history of successes. "Only a small fraction of white immigrants reached the New World under the aegis and at the expense of chartered companies. . . . The age of company-promoted white emigration from Europe was short, over with a few exceptions by the middle of the sixteenth century."[4]

Thus, voluntary settlement for economic reasons was not forthcoming on a large scale in the English colonies or, for that matter, in those of Spain, Portugal, France, or Holland. If settlers came for noneconomic reasons, their progress would be strongly affected by their ability to develop exports and attract capital. But where European demand for American exports was forthcoming—for fish, fur, tobacco, and timber—colonial settlement was scarcely more successful.

McCusker and Menard give an excellent description of the theory that holds that colonial growth was grounded in the export of certain staple commodities. It is worth quoting at length.[5] "Colonization begins with an increase in demand for staples in the metropolis. . . . Given the limited metropolitan supply of natural resources, burgeoning demand produces a sharp jump in staple prices. Those higher prices absorb the high costs of colonial enterprise, raise the rate of return, overcome fears, and increase the incentive to colonize. Capital and labor migrate to the new region, the staple commodity is produced, and trade begins. The metropolis imports the staple and exports manufactures to satisfy the needs of the emigrants. It also exports still more capital and labor to further increase supplies of the commodity."

In McCusker and Menard's version of the theory, equilibrium states are followed by repeated growth cycles, based on new demand shifts or discovery of new staples, thereby continually increasing the size of the colonial economy.

The staple theory story depends upon shifts and elasticity of demand and on the production characteristics of the staple. The European demand for fur and tobacco was inelastic, for timber limited, and the production characteristics of fur and fish made them the enemies, not the progenitors, of settlement.

Overproduction crises plagued tobacco production from the first. Colonial tobacco had to be protected by banning cultivation in Europe. Neither the British nor the French West Indies prospered in the tobacco era, and supply restrictions were enacted well before the middle of the seventeenth century. As Governor Culpeper of Virginia wrote in 1681, "Our thriving is our undoing."[6] The period of growing tobacco exclusively with free labor ended after 1680.

When the demand for tobacco rose after some decades of stagnation, it came not from England but from the continent. Colonial production for this reexport trade responded extraordinarily; it is associated with the spread of slave labor and large plantations. Toward midcentury, tobacco lost its dominance as both great planters and small producers began to diversify into wheat and cattle. Tobacco, which once accounted for almost all the exports of the Lower South, fell to less than 75 percent well before the end of the eighteenth century. As a share of total agricultural production, it was even lower. This staple was weak; with a free labor force it was even weaker.

Fur also suffered from inelastic demand. Before the end of the seventeenth century, beaver flooded Europe in quantities that could not be absorbed at the going price. Quite independent of the state of demand, the fur trade represented the antithesis of settlement. Beaver is not highly re-productive and does not migrate. Once the beaver was exhausted in a locality, the hunters had to move on. Although furs were important to the Pilgrims and Puritans and the early settlers of Virginia, gradually the area east of the Appalachians became denuded of furs. Canadian fur interests reached the Pacific well before the end of the eighteenth century. The fur trade represented dispersion par excellence. In fact, the fur trade drew men away from farming and settled agriculture.

So long as easy prey were available, fur "production" was carried on by hunter-gatherer techniques, not in settled societies. The Hudson's Bay Company, a profitable enterprise over the long run, exemplifies trade without settlement in the clearest way. The company consisted of a handful of Scots and English in stockade forts, who dealt with the Indians, served a tour of duty, and rotated back home. The French too understood that, left alone, fur trading would never result in settlement. It was this conviction that impelled the French minister Colbert to adopt a policy of subsidizing colonization by granting monopolies in return for the promise to colonize. French companies conducted a losing struggle to centralize fur trading at Montreal and Quebec— only then could they collect the revenue to repay the crown for their privilege and make a profit. The traders, of course, wanted freedom to find the best market—it was hard to squeeze monopoly profits out of them without coercion.

Fisheries are another unlikely candidate for initiating settlement. The fishermen of England's West Country managed the industry without settlement and opposed it bitterly. As in the French case, the early colonizing interests were courtiers who sought proprietary monopolies. They could get returns on their investment only by licensing and taxing fishermen. Of course, fishermen would not volunteer for that. Without coercion they would not form settled colonies any more than the coureur de bois would. Only a few thousand people lived in Newfoundland in the eighteenth century; until then there was some doubt about whether it was, strictly speaking, an English colony. Newfoundland had no Anglican church until 1701, no justice of the peace until 1729, and no grammar school until 1799. "The settlement existed largely to serve vessels that came from Europe to buy fish, and became completely dependent on New England for its rum and provisions."[7] If settlers already were established, fish could be an important staple if indeed there was a market for it.

The abundance of timber in America was an important colonial resource. Wood was an especially valuable raw material in preindustrial economies, but American timber products failed to become a major export to Europe because of heavy transport costs. These products benefited from the English wartime demand for ships and masts; generally, however, Baltic supplies dominated the market. American wood products, including ships, faced the same problem fisheries did—there were strict limits on direct trade to Europe because of cheaper alternative European sources of supply. As we shall see, given a closer market, these products (and the services ships could provide) would enter trade on a much larger scale.

Thus neither brigands nor merchants succeeded in founding a permanent colonial economy, and the existence of staple crops was not a sufficient

condition for development—though, as McCusker and Menard have persuasively shown, perhaps it can be regarded as necessary for rapid growth.

The reluctance of Europeans to migrate to the western hemisphere is well
documented. David Ellis has estimated that down to about 1820, four or perhaps even five Africans were brought here for every European who came, and
not until 1840, did European arrivals permanently surpass African. In terms
of immigration, Ellis remarks, the Americas were an extension of Africa
rather than Europe until the late nineteenth century.[8]

Building on the work of Gemery and Galenson, Stanley Engerman notes
that in British North America, two slaves arrived for each white immigrant before the American Revolution. The mainland colonies below the
Mason-Dixon Line received two-thirds of all mainland white immigrants
and nineteen-twentieths of all mainland black slaves. Two-thirds of these
southern white immigrants came as indentured laborers.[9] The flow of transported convicts, vagrants, and defeated rebels has fallen beneath the notice
of historians until recently; some estimates of convicts go as high as 50,000
for 1718–75.[10] How many indentured laborers were kidnapped or shanghaied
or lured by fraud will never be accurately known. But it is clear that only in
exceptional circumstances did large numbers of Europeans desire to emigrate
in the colonial period.

There is no direct relation between migration and population, of course,
since natural increase intervenes. Nor is there a one-to-one correlation between population and labor force, since participation rates and hours worked
must be taken into account. And there is no one-to-one correlation between
labor inputs and development, since capital, technology, industrial organization, and the division of labor must all be considered. In this wider context,
the significance of slavery becomes even more evident.

In 1650, of the nearly one hundred thousand colonists in British America,
there were about 16,200 slaves, all but 1,200 in the British West Indies. The
mainland colonies were 97 percent white and the islands 75 percent white.
By 1750, the mainland colonies were 80 percent white and the islands only
16 percent white.[11] If we calculate the percentage rate of population growth
per decade from 1650 to 1770, we observe the relative blackening of the colonial labor force. The growth rate of the black population exceeded that of
the white for every decade from 1650 to 1750, with two exceptions, 1710–30
and 1720–30, when slave rates were unusually low. In 1750–60, the white
population grew faster than the black one; in 1760–70, they were about
equal; only in the (wartime) decade 1770–80, did white rates decisively pull
ahead (table 2.1).

Table 2.1. Percentage growth rate per decade of black and white populations in British North America

	Black	White
1650–60	122.8	32.3
1660–70	54.8	41.2
1670–80	47.9	19.9
1680–90	33.7	26.0
1690–1700	23.1	16.8
1700–10	53.6	19.7
1710–20	12.0	37.1
1720–30	23.0	31.7
1730–40	42.1	34.1
1740–50	31.2	22.8
1750–60	28.6	35.0
1760–70	29.0	30.7
1770–80	18.8	29.0

Source: Calculated from McCusker and Menard, Tables 5.1, 6.4, 7.2, 8.1, and 9.4, with the assistance of Rebecca M. Solow.

"The blackening of the labor force exceeded the blackening of the population. Participation rates of slaves were higher than those of free whites because of the participation of women and children (among other reasons); slaves worked longer seasons and longer hours, on average, than whites. We know this from direct observation and from the dramatic shift in the labor supply after emancipation, when free blacks had some control over their participation rates and supply of labor.

With an assured labor supply and the emergence of a dependable staple crop, Europeans began to send capital and organize production in America, and the colonies began to grow faster. The staple was sugar." After 1660, England's sugar imports always exceeded its combined imports of all other colonial produce; in 1774, sugar made up just half of all French imports from her West Indian colonies; over the colonial period as a whole more than half of Brazil's exports of goods were sugar. Sugar made up almost a fifth of the whole English import bill in 1774, far surpassing the share of any other commodity. "Already by 1668–9, London's sugar imports exceeded tobacco's by £300,000 to £225,000, and by 1700 sugar imports into England and Wales were twice the value of tobacco."[12]

If the demand for sugar had the characteristics that made a successful staple, were slaves required to produce it? There is no inherent reason why export-led growth is associated with plantation slavery: small holders in West Africa produced most of the world's cocoa crop; small Burmese peasants supplied rice to much of Southeast Asia; the wheat of Canada and the wool of Australia were produced on family farms; but these crops came much later. Sugar had production characteristics that gave slave labor enormous cost advantages over free labor. (The same holds true for colonial rice and indigo. For tobacco and coffee the situation is more complicated and slavery's advantages are less marked.) Thus, the importance of slaves in America was not only that they could be coerced into coming when free labor did not, but when they came they did different things. More of them worked, they worked longer, they could not disperse, they attracted investment, and they produced crops for trade and export on a scale unmatched by free labor. The commodity exports of Britain's American colonies were to a remarkable extent either the outputs of or the inputs into slave colonies as seen in table 2.2.

Slave-grown sugar provided 60 percent of British America's commodity exports. If two-thirds of tobacco exports were slave-grown, the share of slave crops in commodity exports rises to over 78 percent. New England sent 10 percent of its exports to the West Indies. These colonies provided the market for 42 percent of the exports of the Middle Colonies and 32 percent of the nontobacco exports of the Upper South. Without slaves, what would American exports and American markets have amounted to? Without slaves, what would American growth and income have amounted to?

We cannot answer precisely, because we have no reliable estimates of colonial growth rates. Lacking data, income has been estimated by indirection, deduction, and shrewd guesses. Wealth estimates have a firmer foundation. They show that regional variations in wealth are associated with the owner-

Table 2.2. Share of slave colonies in average annual value of commodity exports from British America, 1768-72 (£ sterling)

Total exports		Percent produced by slave labor	Percent exported to slave colonies
British West Indies	3,910.6	Nearly 100	
Upper South	1,046.9	Est. 50	
Lower South	551.9	75	
Middle Colonies	526.5		42
New England	439.1		78
	6,475.0		

Source: Calculated from McCusker and Menard, Tables 5.2, 6.1, 8.2, and 9.3. Canada's small share has been omitted.

Table 2.3. Wealth per free white person in British America, ca. 1770-5 (£ sterling)

Region	Net worth per free white	Total
Continental colonies (1774)	£74	
New England	33	£19,000,000
Middle Colonies	51	30,000,000
Upper and Lower South	132	86,100,000
West Indies (1771-5)		
Jamaica	1,200	18,000,000

Source: For footnotes and explanation, see McCusker and Menard, p. 61.

ship of slaves. McCusker and Menard have summarized the wealth profile of free whites in 1770–5, in table 2.3.

This table seriously understates the share of the British West Indies in the total. Jamaica alone, with a free white population of 15,000, is included; but the total free white population of the West Indian colonies was three times that number in 1770 (McCusker and Menard, p. 54). In 1770, the Leeward Islands and Barbados combined to produce nearly as much sugar as Jamaica. If Jamaica represented two-thirds of the West Indian wealth, the relatively few free whites of the British West Indies would have held more wealth than the New Englanders and perhaps as much as the Middle colonists. The southern colonies held over half the total colonial wealth.

The views on colonial income growth are divided. Pessimists argue that urban and rural poverty were both increasing over the Eighteenth century. Some direct evidence on urban poverty has been offered for Boston, New York, and Philadelphia. For rural areas, strongly rising incomes are hard to imagine, whether we visualize immobile colonists, causing overpopulation and diminishing returns, or mobile colonists, replicating their farms on the frontiers. Some rural poor turned not to the frontier but to vagabondage; some moved to urban centers, depressing incomes there even further. To the extent that there was a safety valve, it only prevented incomes from falling further. A leading pessimist quotes approvingly the conclusion of Terry Anderson: "during the first eight decades of the eighteenth century, agricultural productivity declined [and] real wealth per capita stagnated."[13]

Optimists point to evidence that over this period colonial consumption patterns show marked improvement. From midcentury, the colonies imported a wide range of English manufactured and semi-manufactured goods, which were turning up increasingly in probate inventories north and south. In fact, the colonies were an even more important market for these "baubles of Britain," as T. M. Breen has called them, than the British domestic market.[14]

In a recent article, Main and Main have tried, for New England; to reconcile these improved consumption patterns with the lack of evidence for overall growth in consumption (as measured by the value of probate inventories). They argue "that changes in the makeup of these [consumption] goods constitute an improvement in their material standard of living separate from, and additional to, the growth in total estate value."[15] This improved market basket does indeed argue for increased welfare. Main and Main measure the improvement by using an "index of amenities" devised by Carr and Walsh. The inclusion of imported foods, forks, coarse and fine earthenware, linen, silverware, religious and secular books, timepieces, wigs, and pictures in inventories is taken to show increased economic welfare, independently of total consumption estimates.

These amenities must be investigated further. What share of them did the colonies produce? What proportion was imported? If a large share was imported, how were they paid for? This brings us back by another route to the role of slavery. The tea, coffee, sugar, earthenware, linen, silver, books, docks, and other miscellaneous manufactures the colonists began to consume were not all produced in the colonies; some were imported. Imports had to be paid for by exports, and we know how crucial slave labor was to colonial exports.

McCusker and Menard believe that colonial income growth probably occurred in two spurts. The first took place at the onset of settlement as farms were established in the wilderness; the second, "less pronounced and perhaps less uniform in the several major regions, began during the 1740s, and lasted to the Revolution . . . this second period can be attributed to a burgeoning metropolitan demand for American products, although more-strictly internal processes that reflected a widening market also played a role."[16] The metropolitan demand, we have seen, was mostly for slave-grown products; for some regions, the burgeoning demand was from the West Indian slave colonies.

If we disaggregate and consider the colonies one at a time, slavery looms even larger. In the seventeenth century, Barbados in the Caribbean and Virginia on the mainland were the only colonies of continuous progress. Barbados did not thrive until the sugar/slave era; indeed, no British West Indian colony ever founded a successful society on the basis of free white labor. Virginia was a precarious case of touch-and-go until the tobacco settlement was made. The spread of tobacco merely underlined the hopelessness of establishing a colony on the basis of glass, iron, potash, and wine. Maryland too was poor and thinly populated before tobacco production began. The years of growing tobacco exclusively with indentured white labor were not destined to be many.

If we want to visualize Massachusetts without Boston and its commodity and shipping trade to the West Indies, or Rhode Island without Newport and its slave and rum trade to Africa and the islands, we need only look at Connecticut:[17]

> . . . during the colonial period Connecticut never developed any single center of mercantile and trading interest to compare with Boston: or Newport. The inhabitants of the towns were more or less isolated, their energies were centered largely upon their own agricultural pursuits, and their lives were in the main peaceful and undisturbed. . . . Connecticut stands alone, in a class by herself, as something unique among the British colonies of the New World—a small, slow-moving agricultural settlement, occupying but a tiny part of the earth's surface, largely isolated from the main currents of English and colonial life. . . .

In the eighteenth century, Connecticut, with no banks, no credit, a money shortage so severe that salaries, rates, and taxes were paid in kind, exports few, agriculture primitive and unremunerative, contained 150,000 people in seventy towns that remained substantially without industry as late as 1818.[18]

Similarly, South Carolina and Georgia looked different the minute slave crops appeared. If we want to visualize the Lower South without rice, indigo, and Sea Island cotton, we should think of the backward mixed farms of North Carolina.

Billy G. Smith has written that "Some historians, astigmatised by notions of the shortage of labor, the abundance of natural resources, and the general affluence of early America, have not seen much poverty."[19] They have been "astigmatised" by notions like Hakluyt's and in Adam Smith's that development would be quick and easy.

Colonization Where Land Is Abundant

Adam Smith's optimism rested on the "cheapness and plenty of good land." In settled countries rent and profits eat up wages, but not here. The colonist pays no rent and trifling taxes. He can easily acquire more land than he can cultivate. Indeed, "he can seldom make it produce the tenth part of what it is capable of producing." He will quickly collect laborers and, though wages are high, he will be able to pay them. Of course, his laborers will soon leave him and move on to acquire their own land. Admitting the difficulties of keeping labor, Adam Smith ignores the problem of obtaining it. If rent eats up wages in settled lands, will not wages eat up rent in unsettled ones? The cheaper and more plentiful the land, the harder it is to get the labor; in the limit, it is impossible.

Adam Smith was not really interested in the theory of colonial growth. His concern was the virtues of laissez-faire and in this connection he wanted to show that the gains from the colonies were overborne by the losses inflicted by a mercantilist commercial policy. In fact, until the Colonial Reform movement of the late 1820s, most British writing on colonization was confined to the effects on the mother country and was not concerned with the growth of the colony. The father of the Colonial Reform movement and the pioneer thinker on colonial development was Edward Gibbon Wakefield.[20]

Wakefield turned Adam Smith upside down. Free land did not cause colonial prosperity; it prevented it. Wakefield had ample leisure to reflect. He spent three years in Newgate jail for kidnapping an heiress. Transportation of convicts, colonization, and capital punishment were no doubt prominent subjects of discussion in Newgate, and Wakefield formed strong views on all three. In 1829 he set some of them forth (anonymously) in A Letter from Sydney, purporting to come from Australia but actually originating in Newgate.[21]

Wakefield portrayed himself as a well-to-do Englishman who emigrated to Australia with sizable capital. He planned to buy an estate, build a house for himself, surround it with parks and pleasure grounds, and let the rest of his acreage to tenants, for whom he would also build houses and supply working capital as an English landlord does. He brought twenty thousand acres of land for less than two shillings an acre. The timber that had to be cleared would have fetched £150,000 in England, but for lack of available labor in Australia, the standing timber represented a deadweight loss of £15,000. The absence of labor, of roads, and of towns and markets rendered his coal and mineral deposits valueless, but at least "being under the surface they can do me no harm. An estate of twenty thousand acres, containing rich mines of coal and iron, and covered with magnificent timber, is, no doubt, a very good thing in some countries; but here you will lose money by such a possession."[22] When he tried to sell the estate, people laughed; they could get crown grants at 6d. an acre.

Abandoning his dream of becoming a landed proprietor, he had to try his hand at farming. The servants he brought from England decamped. He supplied their lack with convicts. They lost his sheep and stole his effects. He called a constable and had them arrested and jailed. He called for their release the next day; it was harvest time. Disillusioned with convicts, he sent to his estate in England for shepherds, cowmen, carpenters, and blacksmiths. He paid their passage and promised them wages. The skilled left for higher pay in Sydney; the rest, in a period of two years, saved enough to stock a small farm and, one by one, departed. He ended in a small house in Sydney, paying twice the rent for half as good a house as he could have had in an English provincial town, living off the returns from his English capital and the pitiful proceeds of the sale of his twenty thousand acres.

Countries with abundant cheap land will stagnate, not grow, concludes Wakefield. A poor English farmer can better himself by going to Australia (if he can afford the passage). Higher incomes are to be had, but only as a return to labor. The mere immigration of such people will not ensure economic growth. The immigrants will just replicate their family-sized farms across the vast landscape. Division of labor will be retarded. The surplus of such farms will be small, and there will be difficulties in marketing it. Potential returns to capital *would* be great—rates of return would exceed those current in England—but they cannot be realized without the supply of labor to capitalist landlords that is not forthcoming. No man will willingly continue to share the fruits of his labor with another if he can capture them all for himself.

In Australian conditions, people with capital cannot get labor, few people will come voluntarily, and people with labor who do come cannot easily accumulate or attract capital. "If for every acre of land that may be appropriated here, there should be a conviction for felony in England, our prosperity would rest on a solid basis, but, however earnestly we may desire it, we cannot expect that the increase of crime will keep pace with the spread of colonization," he tells us. "I began to hanker after what, till then, I had considered the worst of human ills—the institution of slavery."[23]

Wakefield understood that the significance of slavery was not that a black labor supply would substitute for a white one, but that slavery under certain circumstances was the sole source of a permanent supply of labor to landlords and the sole source of a sizable accumulation of capital:

> What was the sole cause of the revival of slavery—by Christians, but the discovery of waste countries, and the disproportion which has ever since existed in those Countries between the demand and supply of labor? And what is it that increases the number of slaves of Christian masters, but the increase of Christian capitalists wanting laborers, by the spreading of Christian people over regions heretofore waste?[24]

Wakefield did not, of course, justify slavery but only sought to explain it. His solution to the free land problem was for governments to price land grants and thus prevent the evils of dispersion, lack of markets, and labor and capital shortages. The difficulties of that solution and the history of the Colonial Reform movement are not part of our concern here.

Marx devoted a chapter to Wakefield in *Das Kapital*.[25] He understood well what he and Wakefield had in common—both believed that capital accumulation depended on the private ownership of the means of production. In Marx, this privatization comes about in the transition from feudalism to capitalism, when landlords first acquire property rights in their estates and the power to exclude laborers from them. In America, such property rights exist legally, but because of the extent of land, they are valueless. Both in feudalism and in America, the lack of (valuable) property rights in land means that there is no source of surplus for investment. Modern economists recognize this as a description of the common property case, where all surplus is dissipated and, there is an inefficient allocation of resources.

Wakefield's insights passed into the corpus of classical economics and are probably the origin of the idea, also associated with Merivale, that once empty lands are occupied, slavery will cease. Similar ideas appear in the German historical school and in the work of ethnographers, notably the Dutchman H. J. Nieboer. The modern statement is due to E. D. Domar, who came to the free land formulation from the side of Russian, not American or Australian, history.[26]

Domar presented a simple economic model of an economy with two factors of production, land and labor. He considered two cases: the first where land is limited, the second where land is unlimited. If land is fixed and additional units of labor are added, the resulting additions to output will eventually fall. The landowner will hire labor so long as the output produced by the last laborer hired is greater than the wage he commands. This output produced by the last laborer is less than the average output produced per laborer because of the operation of diminishing returns. Thus the landlord receives the proceeds (revenue) of the average product times the number of laborers, but he incurs as costs only the (lower) marginal product times the number of laborers. The surplus accrues as rent to the landlord.

In the case of unlimited land, as additional units of labor are added, there is no tendency toward diminishing returns. For every laborer there is a plot of land, and the first and last laborers produce the same product. The average product equals the marginal product. In this case, the landlord will find that after he has paid his laborers, there is nothing left over for him. Why would anyone go to work for anybody else if by so doing he earns less than he could on his own? If the landlord pays him what he would earn on his own, there is nothing left over for the rent.

The consequence of this simple model is that where land is free, there will never be a supply of hired labor. If anyone works for someone else, it is by coercion. Free land societies—where the assumptions hold—have either a population of owner-occupied farms or a landed aristocracy and slaves. Of the three elements of this simple agricultural society—free land, free labor, and a landowning aristocracy—only two but not all three will occur. This is the conclusion Domar draws. He does not presume to explain why slavery occurs. Whether slavery is profitable depends on costs and productivity; and whether slavery is introduced depends on the political decision of the state, and this decision, in turn, depends on a host of other factors. Domar is merely pointing to a set of conditions under certain assumptions with certain outcomes and asking us to consider why people will or will not work for other people.

It should go without saying that Domar's model is an abstraction, devised to capture central tendencies, and not a literal reproduction of reality. Land was not literally free. Land having differential fertility or locational characteristics will always command a rent. If the economy depends upon sizable inputs of capital, the model's simple conclusions do not follow. There certainly were positive rents and tenant farmers in colonial America, but the essential nature of the northern colonies was not that of a landed aristocracy and tenant farmers, and the *essential* nature of the southern and West Indian colonies was not that of a free white labor force.

The hypothesis has been around for a long time, Domar concludes; why not invite it in? The first reason to invite it in is that it provides a framework for explaining the choice of social and economic organization that is neither deterministic, simplistic, nor unicausal. Criticisms of the free land approach have been based on substantial misunderstanding. Slavery is not *caused* by free land. Where land is free, slavery *may* or *may not* be more profitable than free labor. This depends on the costs and productivity of both kinds of labor and will vary at different times, in different places, and with respect to different crops. If slavery is more profitable, it *may* or *may not* be adopted; even if profitably established, it *may* or *may not* be abolished. These choices depend on human decisions shaped by political, social, and ideological as well as economic factors. If the assumptions of the model cease to hold, its usefulness is diminished. The advantage of the free land framework is that it points us to those factors that influence the choice of economic and social organization, and these factors, in turn, help explain why at certain times and in certain places such societies choose free or slave labor and what are the consequences of the choice. The free land framework does a better job of explaining the course, pace, and nature of British colonial history than the alternatives. Grounding American exceptionalism in abundant land explains *simultaneously* Turner's frontier and Genovese's South, Jefferson's vision of yeoman agriculture and states' rights and Hamilton's of an industrial society and government intervention. To Jefferson, abundant land meant true democracy. It is the "immensity of land" that enables Americans to avoid the dependence on others that results in "subservience and venality, suffocates the germ of virtue, and prepares fit tools for the design of ambition." Alternatively, the "immensity of land" requires a tariff (or other intervention) to encourage industrialization and prevent the factor combination of cheap land and high wages from keeping America agricultural indefinitely. Wakefield put it succinctly: In the North the tariff, and in the South slavery, prevent America from becoming Jefferson's republic of independent yeomen, a republic that would be incapable of rapid economic development.[27]

Finally, the free land framework directs us to fruitful comparisons among other regions of the world in the same situation. We can understand the relation of the coureur de bois to the Brazilian *bandeirante*, between the American pioneer and the South African trekker, between the Argentine rancher and the Australian sheep farmer, between the American slave and the Australian convict, between the failed Swan River enterprise and the failed East Florida enterprise. The appearance in recent years of books comparing South African slavery with American slavery, the South African frontier with the American frontier, Russian serfdom with American slavery, and Brazilian racism with American racism make the same point. These comparisons are fruitful and enlightening because the free land framework is common to them all. Outcomes differ, but the comparisons are not between apples and oranges but rather between two kinds of apple trees that grow in different ways.

In sum, if we define as the central question of colonial history: "By what methods did Europeans solve the problem of exploiting overseas conquests in regions with abundant land?," we improve our understanding of the peopling and development of colonial British America (and of Latin America, South Africa, Canada, Australia, and New Zealand as well).

Consider briefly the alternative conceptual frameworks that have been offered for the colonial period.[28]

The literature on the economic history of early British America contains two distinct but poorly specified and even contradictory models concerning the relationship between the growth of population and the development of the economy. According to one model, population growth, by expanding the size of the domestic market, permitted specialization, the division of labor, and the capture of various scale economies in the distribution of goods and services and thus promoted development. On the other hand, a classic Malthusian argument is often invoked to describe a process in which population increase pressed against the local resource base and led to diminished yields, falling incomes, declining prospects, and growing inequality, tendencies only partially checked by movements to the frontier.

As McCusker and Menard point out, these interpretations cannot both be right; in fact, neither is helpful. We had indeed colonial development, but not in the way the first suggests and not entirely prevented by the process the second describes.

Consider next an older school of colonial history in the words of its distinguished proponent:[29]

> The men who founded the colonies were Englishmen; the incentives that impelled them to migrate were English in their origin, and the forms of colonial life and government they set up were reproductions or modifications of institutions already established and conditions already prevailing in one way or another at home.

The men who founded the colonies were not all Englishmen; they were not all European; they were not even all men. The incentives of slaves were neither English nor exigent. The forms of colonial life were not modifications or reproductions of the landlord-tenant aristocratic manorial agricultural system so widespread in seventeenth and eighteenth century England—attempts to reproduce that tenure system failed—but consisted of either family farms or plantations, neither of which prevailed at home and one of which was unknown.

Only by viewing the peopling of America as a white Diaspora can we see the transatlantic flow of peoples merely as "an extension outward and an expansion in scale of domestic mobility in the lands of the immigrants' origins" and the form of transatlantic life just as "an exotic far western periphery, a marchland of the metropolitan European cultural system."[30] It will not rescue such conceptual frameworks to add a separate but equal account of a black Diaspora, for the effects of the two flows are not additive but interdependent.

Sustaining old myths requires the invisibility of slavery, and the invisibility of slavery inhibits the development of a better framework for colonial history. Consider next the thoughtful historiographical chapter by Greene and Pole on "Reconstructing British-American Colonial History," which introduces a volume of distinguished essays on the colonial period. In this chapter, the word "slaves" appears just once, the word "slavery" not at all; the subject is not discussed.[31]

The foundation of a satisfactory framework for colonial history, say Greene and Pole, must be based on regional differences. They identify five (or seven) regions and consider several typologies. Island versus continental colonies; southern versus northern colonies; settlement versus exploitation colonies; and farm versus plantation colonies (they prefer the last). If these regions are to be gathered into one comprehensive scheme, they must exhibit significant similarities. Greene and Pole suggest five: (1) each region began as a new society with a common problem of organizing social, political, and economic institutions; (2) each was tied to the Atlantic trading network; (3) all were multiracial and multiethnic; (4) all were characterized by exploitation of the environment and of the peoples living in them; (5) all bore a colonial relation to Great Britain.

The heart of the Greene and Pole approach can be conveyed by the following:[32]

> . . . they were all cultural provinces of Britain whose legal and social systems, perceptual frameworks, and social and cultural imperatives were inevitably in large measure British in origin and whose inhabitants thereby shared a common identity as British peoples living in America. . . . Arguably the most important similarity among the several regions of colonial British America, this common identity imposed upon British Americans in all regions a common set of expectations for their new societies, which they looked upon not merely as vehicles for their own sustenance and enrichment but also as places that would eventually be recognizable approximations of Albion itself. They thus came to the New World expecting, not to create something wholly new, but, insofar as possible, to recreate what they had left behind, albeit without some of its less desirable aspects. Their expectation, their hope, was that the simple societies with which they began would in time develop into complex, improved, and civilized societies as those terms were defined by their metropolitan inheritance.

All the regions in Greene and Pole's scheme, with the common characteristics just identified, are described as having gone through three phases: first, of social simplification of inherited forms; next, of social elaboration of these forms along demonstrably English lines (despite a certain creolization); and finally, of social replication of British society in America, not indeed always harmoniously achieved. Each region went through this developmental framework at different times and with varying results, driven by a tension between the functional imperatives of historical experience and the inherited imperatives of Old World culture.

Ignoring slavery presents serious problems for this story too. Certainly, all of the colonies faced the problem of organizing social, political, economic, and legal institutions: The crucial thing is that they organized them in two distinctly different ways. Whether we look at the forms of immigration, economic organization, social structure, political life, or legal codes, there is a fundamental difference between colonies with free labor and colonies with slave labor. The essential difference between mainland colonies and island colonies, between northern and southern colonies, between farms and plantations, between settlement colonies and colonies of exploitation is the difference between free and slave labor systems. There were very few free men on plantations, in the islands, or being exploited, compared with slaves. The system each region developed was not determined by its geographical characteristics, regionalism qua regionalism. The island societies began with farms and free labor and turned into societies with plantations and slaves; so did Georgia and South Carolina; parts of the Chesapeake changed in the opposite direction. Regionalism doesn't explain development.

Although the colonies had ties to the Atlantic trading system, the nature of their ties differed. Slave colonies sent by far the largest volume of commodities to Europe. Some colonies without slaves joined the Atlantic system by sending commodities to the slave colonies; other colonies without slaves hardly joined the Atlantic system at all; a few did succeed eventually in sending free-grown commodities across the Atlantic.

Of course, all colonists lived to some extent in multiracial and multiethnic environments, but it is naive to pretend that New Hampshire and Antigua are just two examples of this. The world the slaveholders made was not like Vermont or Connecticut, and there is no intelligent sense in which the Pennsylvania farmer and the Jamaican slave shared the same sort of exploitation. The plantation colonies were certainly not "recognizable approximations of Albion"; they were not even recognizable approximations of Rhode Island; and the world found out in 1861 (if it had failed to notice earlier) that the regions of colonial America had not undergone a common development pattern.

Historians—not just black historians—are entitled to ask whether the "perceptual frameworks, and social and cultural imperatives" of *everybody* in colonial America "were inevitably British in origin," and to ask for something better than a continuing homogenization of colonial history that ignores the social, political, economic, legal, and ideological differences between free and slave colonies.

In contrast, the free land framework directs attention to investigating why two streams of labor, voluntary and coerced, came to the colonies and resulted in two different (but interdependent) types of social and economic organization. An approach that skirts this problem violates the facts of history and ignores one of the central issues of the American past.

Notes

1. Adam Smith, *Wealth of Nations*, ed. Edwin Cannan (New York, 1933), 539.

2. This formulation begs the question of how lands became "cheap and abundant." The process of emptying land by the near extirpation of the indigenous population, by disease, by disintegration of their social and environmental fabric, and by dispossession is an ongoing part of the history of these regions.

3. R. B. Wernham, *Before the Armada* (London, 1966), 354, 367–68, quoted in K. G. Davies. *The North Atlantic World in the Seventeenth Century* (Minneapolis, 1974), 27. Davies's book is an indispensable source, and I am deeply indebted to it.

4. Davies, 96.

5. John J. McCusker and Russell R. Menard, *The Economy of British America, 1607–1789* (Chapel Hill, 1985), 21–22.

6. Quoted in Davies, 176.

7. Davies, 165–66; Ralph Davis, *The Rise of the Atlantic Economies* (Ithaca, NY, 1973) 272.

8. David Eltis, "Free and Coerced Transatlantic Migrations: Some Comparisons," *American Historical Review*, Vol. 88, No. 2 (1983), 255.

9. Stanley L. Engerman, "Slavery and Emancipation in Comparative Perspective: A Look at Some Recent Debates," *Journal of Economic History*, Vol. XLVI, No. 2 (1986), 320.

10. Bernard Bailyn, *Voyagers to the West: A Passage in the Peopling of America on the Eve of the Revolution* (New York, 1987), 294.

11. For fuller discussion, see McCusker and Menard, chap. 10; Davis, chap. 8.

12. Davis, 251; Davies, 312.

13. For a good exposition of the pessimist view, from which this quotation is taken, see Billy G. Smith, "Poverty and Economic Marginality in Eighteenth-Century America," *Proceedings of the American Philosophical Society*, Vol. 132, No. 1 (1988), 85–117.

14. T. H. Breen, "Baubles of Britain: The American and Consumer Revolutions of the Eighteenth Century," *Past and Present*, No. 119 (1988), 73–104.

15. Gloria L. Main and Jackson T. Main, "Economic Growth and the Standard of Living in Southern New England, 1660–1774," *Journal of Economic History*, Vol. XLVIII, No. 1 (1988), 27–46.

16. McCusker and Menard, 60, 268–69.

17. Charles M. Andrews, *Our Earliest Colonial Settlements: Their Diversities of Origin and Later Characteristics* (Ithaca, NY, 1933), 117–18.

18. Andrews, 127–9.

19. Billy G. Smith, 108.

20. For an excellent discussion of British economic thought on the colonies in the nineteenth century see Donald Winch, *Classical Political Economy and Colonies* (London, 1965).

21. Edward Gibbon Wakefield, *A Letter from Sydney* in M. F. Lloyd Prichard (ed.), *Collected Works* (Auckland, 1969).

22. Ibid., 103.

23. Quoted in Winch, 95; Wakefield, 112.

24. Wakefield, p. 113.

25. Karl Marx, *Capital: A Critique of Political Economy* (Chicago, 1906), chap. XXXIII, "The Modern Theory of Colonization," 850–66. See also H. U. Pappe, "Wakefield and Marx," *Economic History Review*, 2nd Series, Vol. IV, No. 1 (1951), 88–97.

26. Evsey Domar, "The Causes of Slave: or Serfdom: A Hypothesis," *Journal of History*, Vol. XXX, No. 1 (February 1970), 18–32. Models of economic development with unlimited supplies of labor exist and have even won a Nobel Prize but there is very little literature on the topic of unlimited supplies of land. The exceptions deal mostly in special cases. Cf. Robert E. Baldwin, "Patterns of Development in Newly Settled Regions," *Manchester School of Economic and Social Studies*, Vol. 22 (May 1954), 161–79; Bent Hansen, "Colonial Economic Development with Unlimited Supplies of Land: A Ricardian Case," *Economic Development and Cultural Change*, Vol. 27, No. 4 (1979), 611–27; Gerald K. Helleiner, "Typology in Development Theory: The Land Supplies Economy (Nigeria)," *Food Research Institute Studies* (1966). See also G. S. Callender, "The Early Transportation and Banking Enterprises of the States in Relation to the Growth of Corporation," *Quarterly Journal of Economics*, Vol. XVII, No. 3 (1902), pp. 111–62.

27. Cf. Wakefield, *England and America*, in *Collected Works*, 496 n. "New Orleans is a great market because of slavery; Galena, because of the tariff." For a fuller interpretation of the relation between free land and American political and economic development in the postcolonial period, see the interesting paper by Peter Temin, "Free Land and Federalism: American Economic Exceptionalism," Working Paper No. 481, Department of Economics, Massachusetts Institute of Technology, February 1988.

28. McCusker and Menard, 255. Their dismissal of the free land approach is found on p. 239.

29. Andrews, p. v.

30. Bernard Bailyn, The *Peopling of British North America* (New York, 1987), propositions 1 and 3.

31. Jack P. Greene and J. R. Pole (eds.), *Colonial British America- Essays in the New History of the Early Modern Era* (Baltimore, 1984). Greene and Pole's failure to deal with slavery is remarkable in view of the inclusion of several of the papers in their volume that deal with the subject, especially those of Richard B. Sheridan, Richard S. Dunn, and T. H. Breen.

32. Ibid., 14.

CHAPTER THREE

~

Eric Williams and His Critics

David Brion Davis begins his DuBois lecture by pointing out that slavery antedates written history.[1] Stanley Engerman begins his Louisana State University (LSU) lecture by reminding us that freedom, not slavery, is the peculiar institution and that more slaves left South and Central Africa for North Africa and Eastern Europe than for the Western Hemisphere.[2] Robert Fogel begins his LSU lecture by pointing out that modern American scholarship about slavery derives from the conceptual framework of U. B. Phillips and refuting his paternalistic pro-slavery position. Eric Williams began *Capitalism and Slavery* in an altogether different way.

Capitalism and Slavery begins with the arrival of Columbus in the New World. Williams understood that the twelve million Africans who were sent to the Western Hemisphere constituted the transformative slavery that mattered and that the enslaved dancers and musicians, soldiers and bureaucrats, domestic servants and artisans, harem wives and concubines who were sent elsewhere did not have a comparable impact on world history.

The slave/sugar complex that originated in Mesopotamia and Palestine and came to the New World by way of the Mediterranean islands and the islands off of Africa was transformative in four ways and Williams understood them all.

First, the economic organization of this sugar/trade complex amounted to international agribusiness at a time when Europe was still dominated by feudal premarket systems. In the fifteenth and sixteenth centuries in Madeira and the Canaries and Sao Thomé, land, slave labor, and capital from different places were being combined by profit-maximizing agents to produce a product for further refining that would be marketed all over Europe. Secondly, this slave/sugar complex became the basis for the Atlantic trade: it joined the emptied lands of the New World to the international economy. After the Age of Silver, what moved in the Atlantic were predominantly products to acquire slaves, slaves, the products of slaves, capital and supplies to the slave colonies, and European manufactures bought with the proceeds of these sales. Third, those regions of Europe and America that were linked to the Atlantic trade experienced urbanization and commercialization; regions that lacked this link languished. Fourth, the slave/sugar complex that gave rise to the Atlantic system was the determining factor in the timing and pattern of the birth of the Industrial Revolution in England. The economy characterized by the Industrial Revolution did not depend upon gains from trade in protected markets for economic growth; it depended upon innovation and technological change and a policy of free trade. Finally, Williams held that racism was a consequence and not a cause of slavery, that slavery caused racism and not that racism caused slavery.

When Williams packed for Oxford in 1931, he did not have in his suitcase the tools of modern economic analysis, nor the databases and archival materials that are now available to scholars. What he did have was an original, profound, and comprehensive view of the role of slavery in the modern world. It never occurred to him that he had to controvert the Phillips picture of benevolent slave-owners doing the slaves a favor by bringing them out of Africa and saving them from the horrors of wage labor. He saw slaves not as recipients of largesse, not as victims, but as agents of change. The contribution of Williams must be assessed not by minute examination of his supporting arguments to his insights but by the validity of the insights themselves. Interest in slavery and the Atlantic trade, their impact on industrialization, and the relation of the British West Indian economy to abolition of the slave trade has never been greater, and recent new research has done much to clarify and support the Williams's hypotheses.

Criticism of Williams has come from two sides: first, the denial that the slave/sugar complex made a contribution to the Industrial Revolution in England; and second, that abolition of the slave trade inflicted damage on the British economy that amounted to "econocide." They cannot both be right. If the slave/sugar complex was as insignificant as Williams's critics claim, then abolition of the slave trade could hardly have caused that economy any significant damage. Recent research suggests that both criticisms are wrong and provide support for Williams's hypotheses.

The case that the slave/sugar complex was unimportant in the onset of the English Industrial Revolution is forcefully made by two of the most distinguished scholars in the field. David Eltis and Stanley L. Engerman argue in "The Importance of Slavery and the Slave Trade to Industrializing Britain"[3] that the eighteenth-century slave systems of the Americas were unimportant in the economic development of Europe, and, more specifically, England.

First, they assert that slavery accounts for a small share of the Atlantic trade by measuring the number of slave ships leaving Britain. Does this mean that if the slaves were indigenous they would have had no impact on the Atlantic trade? Second, this omits the contribution to the Atlantic trade of the products of slave economies and the trade of England's New England colonies, nearly 75 percent of whose merchandise and invisible exports were to the Caribbean slave economies and who in turn imported British manufactures with the earnings. It also omits the contribution of the merchant class thrown up by this trade to institutional change in England necessary for sustained economic development.

Next, their argument continues, if western hemisphere slavery led to industrialization, Portugal and Spain would have been the first European countries to industrialize. This is a classic confusion between necessary and sufficient conditions. This argument ignores the fact that Portugal and Spain lacked both the political and economic institutions to develop their colonies and it was only when their colonies were opened to English trade, by the Methuen Treaty with Portugal, by the Asiento, and by the liberalization of Spanish commercial policy, that they were developed. Brazilian sugar and Cuban sugar were developed with English resources. France experienced a spurt of industrial growth during the heyday of Saint Domingue; after the loss of the colony she experienced a period of "repatriation."

While denying the slave-based Atlantic trade a role in the onset of English industrialization, Eltis and Engerman support the Williams view of the subsequent period. Once England became the first industrial nation, her exports were driven by the superiority of her productivity, and she could out compete others on the world markets. This fits the Williams thesis exactly: the industrial England to which the slave/sugar complex contributed no longer needed the protected colonies of the Caribbean to sell their exports. Furthermore, their argument here is a refutation of Drescher's thesis that the abolition of the slave trade inflicted econocide on the British economy: the new industrial economy had no need of the British West Indian colonies; free trade, not protection, was the commercial policy conducive to economic growth. Eltis and Engerman and Drescher are clearly contradictory.

Recent research has provided support for Williams's hypotheses. His case rests on the following arguments: (1) trade matter for industrialization; (2) the Atlantic trade mattered; (3) the Atlantic trade was predominantly slave-based in the seventeenth and eighteenth centuries; (4) this slave-based Atlantic trade was the catalyst for English industrialization; (5) economic distress in the British West Indies facilitated the passage of the Abolition Act of 1807; and (6) industrialized England was better served by a commercial policy of free trade rather than the mercantilist protectionism required to keep the British West Indian colonies afloat.

Contrary to Eltis and Engerman, recent research has argued for the importance of the Atlantic trade for Europe and especially for England. In their article *The Rise of Europe: Atlantic Trade, Institutional Change, and Economic Growth*, Acemoglu, Johnson and Robinson show "that the differential growth of Western Europe during the sixteenth, seventeenth, eighteenth, and early nineteenth centuries is almost entirely accounted for by the growth of nations with access to the Atlantic Ocean, and of Atlantic traders"[4] The profits accruing to these Atlantic traders "enriched a group of merchants who then played a political role in the emergence of new political institutions constraining the power of the crown."[5] Taken together with the economic consequences of the trade, these authors argue that it is "the interaction between critical political institutions and the Atlantic trade" that explains the divergence of England and the Netherlands from Portugal and Spain. Of the countries linked to colonialism and slavery, England developed institutions favorable to economic development. With these institutions, English merchants "invested more, traded more, and sustained economic growth."[6]

In *Why Nations Fail: The Origins of Power, Prosperity, and Poverty*, Acemoglu and Robinson expand these results into a general theory of sustained economic growth. Such growth depends upon a centralized state, not absolutist but with a polity of political pluralism; the establishment of private property; and the rule of law. Again, ". . . relatively small institutional differences in England, France, and Spain led to fundamentally different development paths. The paths resulted from the critical juncture created by the economic opportunities presented to Europeans by the Atlantic trade."[7]

Acemoglu and Robinson agree with Steven Pincus in assigning the accession of William and Mary to the British throne the key role in modeling domestic institutions to favor commerce and manufacturing and foreign policy to foster naval power not territorial armies. Absent the Revolution of 1688, Stuart absolutism would have meant crown monopolization of trade as the monarchy would have resisted the rise of a merchant class as a challenge to its power. Pincus shows that behind the Revolution of 1688, lay the social and economic changes in England due to the flourishing Atlantic trade.[8] He writes, "Atlantic trade provides the only plausible explanation for England's divergence from the European pattern."[9]

No less a personage than Voltaire has anticipated the argument of Acemoglu and Robinson and Pincus: "Trade, which has made richer the citizens of England, had helped make them free, and this freedom, in turn, enlarged trade."[10]

Findlay and O'Rourke, in *Power and Plenty: Trade, War, and the World Economy in the Second Millennium*, while not accepting the Acemoglu and Pincus arguments, nevertheless posit a causal link between trade and the English Industrial Revolution. They write:

> Our first claim is that the remarkable innovations of the Industrial Revolution would not have had the deep and sustained consequences that they did if British industry had not operated within the global framework of sources of raw materials and markets for finished products that had been developed during the heyday of mercantilism and the Navigation Acts, and consolidated by the victories in the long series of wars against the Dutch and French. Slavery and the economy of the New World, supplying first sugar and then cotton, the two major British imports for over two hundred years, was an integral part of this system. The argument is supported by a general equilibrium model linking British manufactures, American agriculture, and the Atlantic slave trade. The New World implied elastic supplies of land, Africa implied elastic supplies of labor; the net effect was an elastic supply of raw materials, implying that the Industrial Revolution drove up raw material prices by far less than would have been the case in a closed economy. In turn this implied that industrial growth could continue for longer without being choked off by input costs.[11]

The role of the slave/sugar complex is illustrated by examining data on British trade prior to the development of cotton. Findlay and O'Rourke quote estimates from Crafts that between 1780 and 1801, increases in exports were equivalent to 21 percent of the total increase of British GNP. This implies an estimate of 46.2 percent in exports of additional industrial output. An even higher estimate is given by Cuenca Esteban: "even as much as 50 to 79 per cent of additional industrial production could have been exported . . . in 1780 to 1801."[12] And an estimate by O'Brien and Engerman suggests that between 1780 and 1801, exports to the Americas accounted for roughly 60 percent of additional British exports.[13] These estimates support the case that for the onset of the English Industrial Revolution the slave-based Atlantic trade was a causal factor. The slave-produced cotton of the American South, which developed later, continued to contribute to sustaining British exports, but the slave trade played no role since the American slave population reproduced itself: the United States had abolished the trade in 1807.

This scenario has been widely accepted, but it has been proposed that without slavery the North American colonies and subsequent United States would have developed the requisite demand for British manufactures with free labor. This counterfactual case encounters serious problems of chronology.

After the Seven Years' War, when the slave/sugar complex was entering its most productive phase, the American colonies were confined by the Proclamation Law to a narrow territory east of the Alleghenies. The products these colonies could offer Europe—timber, fur, tobacco, and fish—were inadequate to elicit a flow of European exports in return. Timber exports competed with European sources; beaver furs were acquired not by settled producers but by hunter-gatherers; the demand for tobacco was inelastic; and Europeans could fish the North Atlantic without forming permanent settlements. The New England colonies provided the significant demand for British manufactures because they found a market for their timber, fish, grain, and other supplies in the slave colonies of the British West Indies.

The Proclamation Law was ended by the Treaty of Paris in 1783, and the Mississippi became the boundary of the United States until the Louisiana Purchase of 1803. In the Jefferson administration settlers began moving to Kentucky, Tennessee, and Ohio. But it was not until the 1820s, with the development of the canal network, that the regions west of the Alleghenies began to be integrated with the regions of the eastern seaboard. The emergence of a free-labor-based American demand for British manufactures in time to set off the British Industrial Revolution in the late eighteenth century is, to say the least, implausible.

It cannot be overemphasized that slaves are not just another item of trade. Slave labor is qualitatively different from free labor: it cannot negotiate the terms of its employment; it can be coerced into more work effort or performing tasks that free labor refuses to do. It was the institution of slavery that joined the Western Hemisphere to the world economy. The classical economists understood that, in a simple economy of land and labor, when land is abundant the owner of land cannot attract a labor force: free labor can move on, acquire land, and retain the full value of its product. As Domar succinctly put it, of the three elements, free land, free labor, and a landowning aristocracy, only two can obtain but not all three. In the North, free labor; whereas in the South, slavery and a landed aristocracy.

The supply of free immigrants to the Western Hemisphere was a trickle compared with the supply of slaves. David Eltis estimates that down to 1820, four or five Africans came to this hemisphere for every white immigrant, and in terms of immigration the Americas were an extension of Africa not of Europe. Where slaves went, commercial relations with Europe and economic development followed; however, where slaves did not go, commercial relations and development languished. Landowners whose labor supply was limited to family labor, apprentices, and a continuing flow of indentured servants could not produce the large-scale staples required for export.

The qualitative difference between free and slave labor can be analyzed in a source-of-growth context. There are two ways to think about slavery in this context. One is simply to treat the advent of black slaves as an increase in the available supply of labor. A variation on this would be to think of black slave labor as a separate input, distinct from other labor. In either case, potential output of the consolidated British Empire is higher than it would be without them, and grows with each successive accretion to the supply of labor. In this way of thinking, there is not much conceptual difference between the acquisition of slaves and the discovery of a mineral deposit or a new stand of timber. In the second variation, there would also be compositional effects: after the advent of slavery, slave-intensive sectors would increase relative to others, just as a new timber-rich discovery would favor wood-using sectors over others. In this way of thinking, an increase in the labor-capital ratio is likely to increase the marginal productivity of capital, and thus the return on investment.

The second way of treating slavery and the sources of growth would go further than the mere increment to the labor supply. This is the Total Factor Productivity (TFP) version: slavery as a method of organizing production enables the same amount of capital and labor (including slaves) to produce a larger output (an aggregate output of higher real value) than was possible without it. This could come about because slaves can be made to work harder than wage-workers or because they can be used in ways that wage-workers cannot to produce high-value output. In either case, real output will be higher than before for the same input of capital and labor (measured in heads). In the working-harder scenario, one might say that a better measure or labor input is "effort," and if labor input is measured this way there is no increase in TFP; we are back to the first way of thinking, and slavery has enabled an increase in the supply of labor-effort. You could still think of this as an increase in TFP, but the increased has occurred through an organizational innovation that allows eliciting more labor-effort. Also in the TFP way of thinking, the marginal product of capital will increase and thus the return to investment.

However any of this is conceptualized, it is an additional fact that slavery reduces the cost of labor to the employer, so that distribution shifts in favor of profits. Presumably part of the attraction of slavery is that slaves can be exploited, that is, "paid" less than equivalent wage-workers.

No part of *Capitalism and Slavery* has been more contested than the argument that the decline of the British West Indies was a causal factor in the Abolition of the British slave trade in 1807. The principal criticism, denying any decline and attributing Abolition solely to Abolitionist ideology and inflicting great, damage to the British economy, was advanced by Seymour Drescher in his extremely influential book, *Econocide*. Subsequent work by David Beck Ryden has presented a challenge to Drescher's work. Williams's assertion of decline derives from the work of Lowell Ragatz, to whom *Capitalism and Slavery* is dedicated. Ragatz's work, *The Fall of the Planter Class in the British Caribbean, 1763–1833*, was published in 1928 by the American Historical Society, and reprinted twice.[14]

Abolition had failed to pass Parliament in the 1790s, when the West Indian colonies were at the peak of their prosperity. The planter interest had no difficulty establishing its importance to the British economy and to the nascent manufacturing interests in particular. By 1807, Ragatz shows, this was all over. The case for decline rests on the loss of the reexport market for Caribbean sugar, increasing duties on sugar to pay for the Napoleonic wars, and the role of the United States shipping interests. What follows is a summary of what Williams would have learned from Ragatz.

The British market had never absorbed all the sugar produced in the colonies; export to European markets through Hamburg was required to take the surplus. By the first decades of the new century, British sugar lost the reexport market. West Indian production was increasing, foreign sales decreased, the market was glutted. This picture is confirmed by Ryden. At the same time the British government, needing revenues to finance the war, raised domestic duties on West Indian production. By 1805, duties amounted to 61.7 percent of the (falling) wholesale price of sugar. The West Indian interests petitioned Parliament and received some relief from these charges.

In addition, the altered role of the former British colonies in North America, now an independent nation, had an important impact on the West Indies. The Navigation Acts were suspended in 1793, so that the Americans could continue to supply the colonies with their vital needs. But British shipping interests objected, and in 1804, the Privy Council supported them against the planter interests, and American imports to the colonies were limited to lumber. Planter opposition was vociferous but useless. By an Act of 1806, imports to the British West Indies by ships belonging to states in amity with Great Britain were allowed for the duration of the war and six months beyond, but all products except lumber and staves must originate in the shippers' country and no sugar or other tropical products could be exported in foreign bottoms. This deprived American shippers of a means of payment for their goods. The Americans retaliated by refusing to sell their supplies except for ready money or bills of exchange, which were in short supply, and the damage to the colonies was drastic.

It would have come as a great surprise to the British planters in the West Indies in 1807, to learn that there was no distress in the colonies. In February 1807, St. Kitts did not have enough food for sale to feed the slaves for a single day. The Leeward Islands were "experiencing a State of Calamity which can scarcely be conceiv'd but by Eye witnesses of it." St. Vincent received in 1807, only a two months' supply of food for slaves. St. Lucia pleaded to be allowed to barter sugar for provisions.[15] American ships were transporting low-cost foreign sugar to European markets at lower shipping rates than the duty-burdened British could match. Average annual exports from Cuba carried by American ships to Europe rose from 85,251 cases in 1780–92 to 175,336 in 1804–1806.[16] In Jamaica, between 1799 and 1897, sixty-five plantations were abandoned; thirty-two sold in chancery to meet claims against them; and there were suits pending on 115 more.[17]

The Abolition of the Slave Trade was a legislative act: it was decided by Parliament and by the political interests and pressure that were brought to bear on Parliament. When Abolition failed in the 1790s, the flourishing British West Indian interests could make a convincing case of their great importance to the nation's economy. That case had collapsed by 1807: the West Indian interests were coming hat in hand to Parliament, seeking relief on the basis of their former contribution. The newly-acquired underdeveloped colonies had no voice in the debate. By 1807, the Abolitionists were pushing against an open door. The decline of the British West Indies played a causal role in the Abolition of the Slave Trade

That is the micro-argument for the role of decline in Abolition. There is also a macro-argument and it goes like this: the new economy that the slave/sugar complex initiated had no need of a protectionist commercial policy and would benefit from free trade; the colonies needed protection but abandoning protection would no longer be costly to England and retaining it would be.

In the eighteenth century, British naval and military superiority in wars against the Spanish, the Dutch, and the French, enabled her to assemble an Atlantic empire comprising Britain, Africa, the British West Indies and the North American colonies in a large free trade area sheltered by barriers to outsiders. The institution of slavery helped build the Atlantic trading system in three ways: slavery joined the western hemisphere to the international trading system; without slavery, no large-scale tropical staple exports to England; without slavery, no significant exports from New England; without New England demand, less demand for English manufactures. Doubtless there would have been an Atlantic trading system without slavery, but its timing and pattern and consequences would have been different.

England had the right political and economic institutions to exploit these opportunities. With the encouragement to English manufactures, England became the world's first industrial nation. With her comparative advantage in manufacturing now established, she had no need of a protectionist commercial policy, and free trade was more advantageous. The old policy had made its contribution and was no longer needed: protectionism prevents comparative advantage from determining patterns of trade and is costly to economic development.

There is a tendency among historians of Abolitionism to view its history as autonomous and independent of economic and social developments. This is especially true of Seymour Drescher, who in *Econocide* appears to see the causal explanation of Abolition as a battle between ideology and economic determinism, and ideology wins by a knockout. From the Williams point of view, Abolition and Emancipation can only be understood as the interaction between ideology and changed economic conditions and changes in the social structure of English society.

In the late eighteenth century, England began to move from a rural agricultural society with a polity based on Crown, Church, and the Landed Aristocracy toward an urban industrial society with a limited monarchy, religious diversity, and a democratic franchise. No longer a society dominated by the establishment of Church and Landlords, there arose a wider population of Dissenters, manufacturers, artisans, and workers. Victorian historians like G. Kitson Clark have argued that these new forces had economic power but no political representation in the unreformed Parliament. They had to show their strength by extra-Parliamentary pressure, by mass meetings, petitions, and boycotts. They needed issues to display on their banners, and one of the convenient issues was Abolition. However upper-class its leadership, Abolition found its rank and file support among the new social classes the economy had begun to throw up. The Abolitionist movement can thus be seen as the result of the interaction between ideology and social and economic change.

That racism is a consequence and not a cause of slavery is borne out most clearly by the American experience. The clearest explanation of this is given by G. Edward White in *Law in American History Vol. 1, From the Colonial Years Through the Civil War*.[18] In seeking to recover the legal and cultural architecture of slavery, White writes, "One needs to bear in mind that American slavery was a unique institution. Although slavery existed in other nations . . . its 'transplantation' to British Colonial America resulted in its being singularly grounded in race. Only nonwhite persons could become slaves, and the status of slaves was inheritable."[19] Only this slavery equated the status with race.

White goes on to explain that there was no English common law defining slavery. England had established that none of her citizens could be held as slaves, so the legal and cultural architecture of slavery remained to be developed. Until the widespread adoption of slavery as an industrial system, fluid relations among slaves and white indentured servants were common. Once plantation slavery was adopted as a profitable economic institution, the legal and cultural architecture was put into place, and slaves were deprived of rights and subject to disabilities. But the economic institution preceded the legal.

In summary, White writes, "The role of American legal institutions was largely to sustain [the] dimensions of slavery rather than to create them . . . law helped define the status of slavery and the persona eligible for it. But these definitions occurred after African-American slavery had already been established."[20] Racism was not the cause of slavery: slavery was the cause of racism.

White's work also supports the view that the rise of Abolitionism was not an exogenous development but was intimately connected with events in the economy. He points out that until the 1830s, slavery was not a divisive issue in the United States and there was widespread consensual agreement on the subject. The consensus rested on four points: First, slavery was widely seen as a necessary evil, inconsistent with human rights, but confined to imported African captives. Second, it was widely expected that slavery would die out. Third, since the institution antedated the Declaration of Independence and the Constitution, the federal government had no power to abolish it. Only the states had that power. Fourth, so long as slavery was limited to the production of tobacco and rice and indigo, and modest amounts of sea-island cotton, it could reasonably be seen as a local issue unlikely to persist. After the 1830s, these assumptions ceased to obtain and the consensus broke down.

Eli Whitney's invention of the cotton gin transformed slave production beyond its modest limits, and at the same time the westward movement of American population meant that slavery was no longer a minor local interest. In this situation, White explains that pro-slavery interests perceived that the institution, far from being a local matter, had potential for limitless growth. Anti-slavery interests saw that in this situation the institution had to be eliminated everywhere in the country. The ideological split was brought on by the enhanced profitability of slavery on the one hand and the westward movement of the population on the other. The resulting history of Secession and Civil War can be seen in the context of the interaction between ideology and historical developments.

The fugitive slave, White continues, became the symbol of the tension between Property and Liberty that slavery posed. Reaction to Chief Justice Taney's decision in the Dred Scott case, the ultimate racism, defining blacks as unfit to associate with whites and having no rights of citizenship, precipitated the dissolution of the Union.

For Williams, slavery was not just about seizing twelve million Africans, transporting them to the Western Hemisphere, and coercing their labor and their lives. It was also about creating an international trading system that was the catalyst of English industrialization. It was also the origin of American racism that persists to this day.

Notes

1. David Brion Davis, *Challenging the Boundaries of Slavery*, (Cambridge, MA, Harvard University Press, 2003).

2. Stanley Engerman, *Slavery, Emancipation, and Freedom: Comparative Perspectives*, (Baton Rouge, LA, State University Press, 2007).

3. "The Importance of Slavery and the Slave Trade to Industrializing Britain," *Journal of Economic History*, Vol. 60, No. 1 (March 2000), 123–44.

4. "The Rise of Europe: Atlantic Trade, Institutional Change, and Economic Growth," *American Economic Review*, Vol. 95, No 3, June 2005. (op. cit., 546. Italics in original.)

5. op. cit., 567.

6. op. cit., 572, (italics in original).

7. *Why Nations Fail: The Origins of Power, Prosperity, and Poverty* (New York: Crown Publishers. 2012).

8. *1688: The First Modern Revolution* (New Haven: Yale University Press, 2009).

9. See the review of Pincus by Bernard Bailyn, *New York Review of Books* (November 19, 2009), 45.

10. See Ronald Findlay and Kevin H. O'Rourke, *Power and Plenty: Trade, War, And The World Economy in the Second Millennium*, (Princeton: Princeton University Press. 2007), 347.

11. op. cit., 342.

12. op. cit., 345.

13. Ibid.

14. See *The Fall of the Planter Class in the British Caribbean, 1763–1833*, (1928) by the American Historical Society, reprinted in 1963 by Appleton-Century-Crofts, and reprinted in 1971 by Octagon Books division of Farrar, Straus & Giroux.

15. Ragatz, op. cit., 302–03.
16. op. cit., 309.
17. Ragatz, op. cit., 308.
18. G. Edward White *"Law in American History Vol. 1, From the Colonial Years Through the Civil War* (Oxford and New York, Oxford University Press, 2012).
19. op. cit., 296.
20. op. cit., 299.

CHAPTER FOUR

~

Why Columbus Failed:
The New World without Slavery

Historians commonly tell two different stories about the impact of the discovery of the New World, and neither story survives close attention to the
historical record. One says that Europe brought the backward primitive regions of the Western hemisphere out of darkness into the ambit of European
civilization when European settlers came with their culture and technology,
and mutually advantageous economic development ensued. The other story
says that European civilization despoiled the societies and ecology of the
New World, impoverishing them and enriching itself at their expense. I
shall argue that the development of the Western hemisphere was difficult,
delayed, and by no means automatic; that although Europeans did indeed
despoil the New World, that is not how they enriched themselves; and that
it was the importation of millions of African slaves that initially allowed Europe to profit from her conquests and allowed settlements to take hold and
grow. Enduring profitable relations between Europe and the Americas were
founded on the institution of slavery, and the labor of Africans made possible
the exchange of primary products for manufactures which characterized these
relations in the colonial period.

　　How can one society gain economically from the military conquest of
another? By plundering and looting; by engaging in legitimate trade and
investment; or, if the conquerors want more than the earnings of legitimate
trade and investment—and that is what we mean by exploitation, by forcing
unfair terms on the conquered. This is how the Portuguese, Dutch, French,
and English managed their relations with Asia and Africa from the sixteenth

century. But if there is little to loot and little traditional trade to participate in or dominate, then how can the conquerors gain? Europeans must then found an economy, someone must volunteer to come and work, someone must send or generate capital, and trade connections must be established. This is no easy task.

Europeans faced intrinsic difficulties in exploiting the Western hemisphere and were struggling unsuccessfully until the advent of slavery. The Atlantic trade that joined the Old and New World in the colonial period was almost totally dominated by commerce in slaves, the products of slaves, the flow of capital and supplies to slave economies, and commodities bought with the proceeds from supplying these economies. Europe did benefit significantly from the discovery of America, but not without the labor of millions of slaves, overwhelmingly black Africans: had that labor not been available, economic development would have been halting and growth retarded. Let me illustrate the difficulties facing Europeans in the New World by retelling the story of "Spain's Failure to Profit from Columbus's Discoveries" in the West Indies, in the first section. We can then consider the underlying reasons for this failure in the second section entitled: "Underlying Reasons for Failure," and relate them to the struggles of other European nations to establish profitable colonies in the third section: "Other European Nations Struggle to Create Profitable Colonies." Finally, we consider why and how the introduction of slavery eventually enabled Europeans to found successful American empires in: "Slavery and the Founding of American Empires."

Spain's Failure to Profit from Columbus's Discoveries

The agreement that Columbus signed in April 17, 1492, with Ferdinand and Isabella bestowed on him hereditary admiralship and specified that of all the merchandise of "pearls, precious stones, gold, silver, spices," or other things "of whatever name, kind, and description," he found there, he could retain a tenth of the net value and an eighth of the trading profits. It was the gold that mattered. Kirkpatrick Sale has counted the occurrence of the word oro in Columbus's Journals during the first voyage: twenty-three times in the Bahamas, nineteen times along Cuba and ninety-eight times in Hispaniola.[1] Sale claims that "in every book [in Columbus's library] he commented on the regions of and traffic in gold and underlined almost every reference to it two or three times."[2] Another source counts sixty-five mentions of gold in Columbus's diary during the first Atlantic crossing.[3] The Spanish planned to barter trinkets for gold and ultimately to find its source.

Bartering for gold brought disappointing results, and gold placers were found only on Hispaniola, but that was enough to insure a second voyage.

The policy this time added settlement to the acquisition of gold. The Crown agreed to individual private ownership of land in the colony; still, two-thirds of the plan for the voyage was devoted to describing the conditions for gathering, smelting, storing, selling, and shipping gold. The settlers, soldiers, farmers, artisans, and adventuresome gentlemen of means would be granted land on condition that they cultivate specific crops for four years and build themselves homes and flour and sugar mills. The problem of keeping settlers from plunging headlong to a gold rush, and neither providing food nor remitting their share to the authorities, was to be met by confining mining to certain times of the year.

Nor did this plan succeed, neither settlement nor the acquisition of gold. Hunger, illness, and disaffection afflicted the settlers, and the natives grew hostile. Columbus tried yet another policy. He levied tribute in gold (or cotton, later cassava) on all male Amerindians of a certain age. Unable or unwilling to meet the demands, some natives fled, and those who remained were enslaved. The ruin of the indigenous economy was in train, and famine and depopulation slowly spread across the land. Neither gold nor any other produce poured into Spain, and enslaved Amerindians were the export crop that paid for supplies. Columbus returned home, this time to no honors.

Ignored by Ferdinand and Isabella for two years, Columbus was at length permitted a third voyage, reduced now to the companionship of convicts. He found matters no better on Hispaniola. A group of colonists under Francisco Roldán had rebelled against his brother, whom he had left in charge. Columbus found the rebels well established. Less interested in exploiting the island for the Spanish at home than in living well in an Hispano-Amerindian state, Roldán at first made allies of the natives.

Ultimately Columbus was forced to make an accommodation with the rebels, initiating still another change in policy. Roldán's demand was to reward the Spaniards not with land but with the services of Amerindian labor. Instead of territorial domains, the Spanish were to receive a native community, under its chieftain, to work in mines, in agriculture, and to perform services. Under this arrangement, then, many settlers simply dispersed over the island to take up their assigned repartimientos and live self-sufficiently on the labor of the natives. The rest grew increasingly restive under Columbus' family rule. The situation moved Ferdinand and Isabella to supplant Columbus, and he left the island in chains early in October 1500.

For the epitaph of the Spanish incursion into the West Indies, we cannot improve upon the words of David Watts. I have stopped my sketch before the brief fourth voyage and the regimes of Bobadilla and Ovando.

Long before the end of the sixteenth century, large areas of the Greater
Antilles, and virtually all of the Lesser Antilles and the islands north of the
Venezuelan coast, had been abandoned by the Spanish to the re-growth of
secondary forest and scrub, and to the naturalized herds of hogs, cattle and
horses that still remained . . . The Indian populations had long gone, except
in Trinidad and a very few of the lesser Antilles, which had received minimal
attention from the Europeans. In particular, the stable, prosperous, welcom-
ing, agriculturally sophisticated Arawak domains in the Greater Antilles
had been destroyed completely, to make way for an ultimately small and
predominantly transient Spanish population and many more negro slaves,
living in what after 1519, was a fringe, supporting region for Spanish interests
on the mainland.

Underlying Reasons for Failure
The point of this vastly oversimplified sketch of Columbus's career in the
West Indies has been to draw attention to the intrinsic difficulties facing
a European power in its efforts to exploit conquered lands in the Western
hemisphere.

When Europeans discovered the sea route to Asia, they found populous,
superior civilizations, producing metalware, textiles, porcelain, and spices, in
a sophisticated trade network centuries old. Europeans wanted these commodities enough to bear the cost of transporting them; Asians wanted less of
European goods, not because they could not afford them, but because their
needs were being met by Asian production and exchange. Asia was willing,
however, to accept bullion, and the trade was balanced in that way. In the
New World the Europeans found widely separated economies, sufficient
for their own purposes, but lacking an array of incentives, institutions, and
an economic life readily available for European participation. The seeds of
Spanish failure in the West Indies lie in these fundamental conditions, and
all subsequent European imperial powers faced the same difficulties and the
same potential failure.

Initial efforts at barter were doomed by the Western hemisphere's in-
ability to provide, or keep providing, commodities for trade. Policies of loot
and tribute are inherently costly to maintain and are likely to be counter-
productive in the long run. No incentive exists for the exploited to provide
the tribute (quite the contrary, they are incentives to evade), and when the
accumulated assets run out, they will not be voluntarily resupplied. Where
land is available to the natives, they will do better to flee than to remain.

· Sending settlers is no solution either. Few settlers volunteer for the risk
of moving to an unknown wilderness, and if any come they work on their

own account and are unwilling to provide profits for European companies or individuals. Europeans who found self-sufficient economies, whether North American farmers or Latin American ranchers, provide no profits for Europeans and attract no capital from them.[4] If barter, tribute, and settlement are unlikely to succeed as strategies of exploitation, what can be done? Grants of land to private individuals will be valueless unless there is an accompanying supply of labor. This was as obvious to Roldán and his followers as it is to us. Neither Europeans nor Amerindians will volunteer to share the fruits of their labor with European masters if by moving to the frontier they can retain these fruits for themselves if the European landowner is to acquire a labor supply it will have to be by coercion.

We have seen in the West Indies that as the Spanish forced the Amerindians to produce the export crops they wanted, they imposed insupportable burdens on the natives. Without increased productivity they could no longer produce for the Europeans and supply food as well. The more the Europeans squeezed the more the natives sickened and died.

The official Spanish census counted six hundred thousand natives on Hispaniola in 1508. Estimates of the original population vary widely, from one hundred thousand to seven or eight million. Watts prefers las Casas's contemporary estimate that three million died between 1497 and 1508. The depopulation antedated the introduction of smallpox and is attributable in Watts's view to the disruption of the native economy.[5] In the conditions that prevailed, it is almost true to say that there was no quick way for the Spanish to exploit their Caribbean conquests.[6]

Other European Nations Struggle to Create Profitable Empires

In 1504, when Cortes arrived in Hispaniola, he announced that he had not come to till the soil like a peasant. No one else would voluntarily come and till the soil for him either. Wherever land is freely available its price will be at or near zero; the returns will be garnered by labor; and if the Corteses of the New World want the returns without performing the labor they will have to lay ownership not to worthless land but to valuable labor. They failed to do this in the West Indies, and they failed to exploit the islands successfully. Every colony in the Western hemisphere struggled with Cortes's and Columbus's problem; let us consider them one by one.

Mainland Spanish colonies. If Spain failed to profit by her dominion over the West Indies, did she profit from her mainland possessions?

Spanish policy here was limited to the extraction of precious metals, and colonial settlement was confined to the mining areas and the necessary supply and transport routes. The proportion of bullion in the total value of exports from Latin America may have been well over 75 percent in most of the colonial period. But the imperial gains were temporary at best and illusory at worst. They were over by the beginning of the seventeenth century, when Spain fell into a deep depression, from which she did not recover until late in the eighteenth century. The reappearance of the Spanish empire as an important player in international trade would have to await the introduction of African slaves on a large scale into the cane fields of Cuba at the end of the eighteenth and beginning of the nineteenth century.

The link between bullion imports and Spanish economic activity was described by Huguette and Pierre Chaunu on the basis of detailed evidence of shipping between Seville and the colonies.[7] Between 1504 and 1550, an influx of bullion stimulated Spanish investment and imports, then a slump of a dozen years followed. After the Treaty of Château-Cambresis in 1559, ending the war with France, trade resumed, and the imports of silver into Spain were answered by exports or Spanish goods, "Finally, at the beginning of the seventeenth century, saturation point is reached. The colonial market for European goods has reached the limits of its expansion; and from about 1622, with American demand falling off, silver reaches Seville in diminishing quantities, Seville's Atlantic trade slumps decisively in value and volume, and Europe enters its depression of the mid-seventeenth century."[8]

Total imports of bullion peaked in the decade 1591–1600, at seven million pesos de minas, stayed at a little more than five million for the first three decades of the new century, and fell precipitously in the 1630s and 1640s, to just over a million in the 1650s. From the 1630s, the decline was "steep, continuous and unmistakable."[9] Bullion imports peak in the 1590s, remain stable at a slightly lower level until the 1630s, when the steep decline sets in. Watts's figures are modified from H. Kamen.[10]

The number of official sailings from Spain to America fell from about thirty in the 1590s, to a level rarely exceeding forty in the 1650s, with some years showing fewer than twenty; sometimes warships outnumbered merchantmen.

The Chaunu data are based on Seville and are by now outdated. To assess the impact of mainland Spanish colonies we must look at the entire production of precious metals and see what happened to it. Although gold was mined, sometimes in large quantities, silver always predominated in volume and value, and we limit our attention to silver. Recent scholars have relied on royalty accounts on coinage to estimate silver production. Peter Bakewell, presents a synthesis of estimates in his article on mining in the Cambridge History of Latin America.[11] Since some bullion must have escaped paying royalties, Bakewell views his data as minimum estimates, valid for long-run trends. (The estimates remain tentative for other reasons as well.)

Bakewell explains that silver was found at great heights, often in rain forests, with rich: ores above and below the water table. The sulfide ores below were less easily refined and liable to flooding. Mining was a lottery with a few large winners and many losers. "If the vein was lost, or workings suddenly flooded, then a mine could swallow silver as quickly as it disgorged it. Creditors closed in, seizing land, houses, belongings. Few families, indeed, remained prosperous in mining for more than three generations."[12]

Bakewell's charts show that Spanish colonial silver mining was dominated by the large mines of two regions: New Spain (Mexico) and the Chile-Peru-Charcas (Bolivia) region. Potosi produced half the Spanish colonial silver in the last quarter of the sixteenth century. Production reached a peak in 1592, and was the highest of any mining center in the entire colonial era. But by 1600, Potosi entered a period of decline lasting 130 years.

The output of the large mines of New Spain[13] fluctuated about a steady plateau until about 1730, when a gradual rise began. The large production of the mines of New Spain is a phenomenon of the late eighteenth century, especially after 1780. The production at the Valenciana mine at Guanajuato, the largest single mine ever worked in colonial Spanish America, peaked between 1780 and 1810. Behind this boom, Bakewell especially cites an abundance of mercury for refining (reversing earlier trends) and the introduction of blasting for underground exploration.

The profile of total production then is of the early predominance of Potosi, its 130-year decline after 1600, and the subsequent rise of the New Spain centers, gradually in the Middle of the eighteenth century and strongly at its end: a U-shaped curve centering on 1730.

This silver flowed in two directions, across the Atlantic to Spain and across the Pacific to Manila. At the peak of Potosi's production the two flows were approximately equal, and Crown efforts to prevent the Manila trade remained a dead letter.[14] The trade continued until the British captured Manila in 1762.

The mining era was ill-suited to initiate sustained growth, in the New World. For the mining regions, the economic effects of silver production do not differ from those of any other commodity. Men are employed, income is generated. Economic activity was spurred in the Chile-Peru-Charcas region at the end of the sixteenth century, and in New Spain, at the end of the eighteenth. The former imported only a trickle of goods from Spain via the Isthmus, more from the Orient. Mexican mining towns imported cloth, wine, and iron from Spain, slaves from Africa, and silks and spices from the Orient. In both places local activity was stimulated to provide grain, cattle, textiles, and crafts. The towns contained magnificent Baroque churches, but in some respects resembled mining towns everywhere. At its peak Potosi boasted 700–800 criminals, twenty white prostitutes, four gambling houses, and four dance halls.[15]

The mining booms were widely separated in distance and in time and occurred in isolated settings. In northern New Spain, the Charcas altiplano, and northern Chile, they were almost the only Spanish settlements. This limited their linkages to the rest of the economy.

More than a century separated the peak activity in Chile-Peru-Charcas from that in New Spain. The result was a long period of weak economic ties between Spain and her colonies, so weak that the transatlantic system was brought to the verge of collapse by the middle of the seventeenth century. The colonies looked inward to latifundia development, Spain herself was in a state of "sheer prostration."[16] The revival of the late eighteenth century came with the opening of the Spanish empire to the countries of northern Europe, and by this time the mining regions had lost in relative importance to the slave-sugar and tobacco industry of Cuba and to other economic developments in Chile, Argentina, and Uruguay.

The effect of bullion imports into Spain depended on their use in the economy. In Spain bullion is more than an ordinary commodity, it becomes part of the money supply and affects wages and other prices.

Perhaps as much as 60 percent of Spain's silver imports were remitted abroad. Some portions were retained, providing outdoor relief for the Castilian aristocracy, enabling some of its members to retire debt, acquire property, or facilitate family settlements. Silversmithing flourished as no other industry. The majority of the silver left Spain as the price level rose, making exports expensive and imports cheap. Scholars have long debated the role of bullion imports in the inflation of the sixteenth century, but, whatever the real causes, the influx could only have exacerbated the rising price level.

The Spanish thus supplied their American colonies from northern European sources and paid in specie. They paid for imports from the East in specie, and they financed their extensive wars by specie. Bullion flowed to Amsterdam, to London, to German bankers, to the east via the Dutch and English East India Companies. A conduit for silver, Spain herself had to rely on a copper coinage compound by the end of the sixteenth century.[17]

What did the European nations do with the silver? There is substantial agreement that western Europe at this time (say, 1550 to 1800) exported about as much bullion as it received.[18] The destinations were the Baltic countries, the Levant, and the Orient. Kindleberger thinks that the Baltic countries may have hoarded as much as 40 percent of its imports, circulating 20 percent back to the West in spending on luxuries and travel and 20 percent on to the East. The Middle East absorbed some in hoarding, but for the most part passed it on eastward. Silver exchanged for Asian textiles, spices, coffee, and silks at Ormuz on the Persian Gulf and Mocha on the Red Sea. Once the specie reached India and China, much of it disappeared into hoards and never circulated further. Kindleberger makes a persuasive case that the traditional view of the Far East as a sink for bullion is substantially correct.

The bullion era did not initiate sustained economic growth for either Spain or her colonies, and, aside from Holland, the late sixteenth and seventeenth centuries were years of crisis for Europe. The silver of colonial Spanish America apparently facilitated trade with the Baltic and the Middle East and was exchanged also for the luxury goods of Asia. Much of it entered the hoards of India and China, and some of it was taken out of circulation and hoarded at every step of the journey east, in the Baltic and in the Middle East. The recovery of mining production in the late eighteenth century faded in importance compared with other developments in the western hemisphere. "By 1789 the produce shipped from the French colony of Saint Dominque came close to equalling the value of the exports of the entire Spanish empire in the New World."[19] The exports, Brading adds, were produced by a slave population of some four hundred and fifty thousand; there were 4.5 million inhabitants of the Spanish colonial empire.

In Brazil settlement succeeded where sugar plantations took hold, and sugar expansion succeeded as African labor replaced Amerindian. Discovered in 1500, and at first neglected, Brazil presented limited opportunities for barter to the Portuguese seamen and traders who first arrived: they found monkeys, parrots, and dyewood. The Crown authorized settlement in 1534, to hold the colony against the French, hoping that gold would eventually be found. King Dom Joao established twelve hereditary captaincies between the Amazon and Sao Vicente, from thirty to a hundred leagues wide and extending indefinitely into the interior. The grantees were to found townships and were given rights of taxation on all commodities except Brazil wood (retained as a Crown monopoly), the right to tithes on fish and sugar, and the right to license buildings and mills. Who would settle these captaincies and who would supply the labor for the Portuguese who planned to profit from them? No serious attempt was made to settle the four most northernmost captaincies; in six others, settlement was tried and abandoned. Just as in the Spanish Caribbean, settlers could devise no means of survival, and they faced the hostility of the indigenous people. In the South, in Sao Vicente, the Portuguese intermarried and integrated into the native society, living among the people quite apart from any European settlement.

In 1549, a new captaincy was established at Bahia, and, despite Crown prohibition, the settlers began to enslave the Amerindians. This enslave-ment has been described as a passing moment in Brazilian history, but it was a long moment with a complex story, admirably told by Stuart Schwartz.[20] Struggles among Jesuits, Crown, and colonists resulted in resistance, rebel-lion, famine, and disease among the natives. In the early period of settlement (1550s and 1560s), plantation workers were virtually all Amerindian; in the 1560s, Schwartz estimates Pernambuco's labor force at a third African slaves (page 65); but when the rapid expansion of the Brazilian sugar economy oc-curred at the end of the sixteenth century and the first two decades of the seventeenth, the shift to African labor was decisively underway, as their superior productivity was recognized and they became affordable.

Just as in the case of Brazil, the Caribbean economies flourished only in the sugar era, and the sugar era depended on slaves. The British began to settle in the West Indies at about the time they came to mainland North America. As Spanish power declined, the out-islands of the Lesser Antilles were abandoned by the Spanish, and French and English colonists moved in: the English to St. Kitts (1624), Barbados (1627), Nevis (1628), and Montserrat and Antigua (1630s). The original settlers found no natives on Barbados and were unable to utilize the fierce Caribs as a labor supply else-where. There was not much question of barter or Amerindian slavery. Once the land was parceled out, the problem of labor supply remained. The islands were not especially attractive to Englishmen, and much of the white servant population was drawn from the impoverished Irish peasantry. There were slaves in the economy, but it was not yet a slave economy. The islands all began with small white landholders farming with an indentured servant and a slave or two. The population clustered along the islands' shores. One crop after another was tried and failed, and efforts to clear inland areas were not seriously undertaken. Tobacco, the principal crop, proved unprofitable, and cotton, ginger, and indigo did not succeed either. The white population of the West Indian colonies reached a peak in the 1640s, and the consequences of economic failure were famine, disease, and emigration. Some settlers turned to buccaneering, or vain attempts at other islands, and some died at the hands of the Caribs.

The pre-slave era in the British West Indies was not a success. "By 1640 it was obvious that Barbados was in a decline . . . colonists also began to leave St. Christopher in droves by 1640 . . . in 1642 Governor Ashton of Antigua reported to the Earl of Carlisle that the island was actually running to ruin." In not one of the Caribbean islands did the English inhabitants succeed be-fore 1650, in establishing a viable white society: on the contrary, "economic

and social conditions in the oldest colonies created the greatest concentration of poverty-stricken freemen in any of England's dominions before
1776."[21] Barbados would have to wait another generation for slavery to make
it the richest British colony; the others would have to wait even longer.[22]

French West Indian history parallels British. Colonies failed in their
pre-slave era and thrived during slavery. St. Kitts was the mother island of
the French as well as of the British West Indies. D'Esnambuc and de Roisy,
probably pirates, established a colony there in 1625, sharing the island with
the English. Ten years later the French branched out to Guadeloupe and
Martinique, subsequently moving north to St. Martin and St. Eustatia with
the Dutch, and south to Maria Galante, the Saintes, and Grenada.

For the French too, tobacco was the only crop with a market sufficiently
robust to earn capital and supplies for successful colonization. Again, the
Dutch managed the initial development, bringing German grain, Dutch
manufactures, and Irish salt beef, and taking away tobacco for European distribution. But French West Indian tobacco faced the same over-production
problems the British did: demand was inelastic, and as production increased
and prices fell, quantity demanded did not respond proportionately. In 1639,
the French and English governors on St. Kitts agreed to restrict tobacco
production by limiting planting to alternate years. Settlers were encouraged
to try cotton, roucou, later indigo, but these never caught on. The French
islands remained outposts of impoverished tobacco farmers for another
twenty-five years.

The introduction of a slave-sugar economy began with a few mills in
the hands of rich planters on St. Kitts and Martinique in 1658. Most small
farmers lacked the resources to grow sugar themselves and would not grow
it for the large landowners. By the middle of the 1660s, sugar production
dominated tobacco, but the islands contained only a small number of large
slave-owning planters and a large number of poor white tobacco farmers. Just
as the initial success of the slave-sugar economy in Barbados was followed by
a long lag before expansion elsewhere in the British islands, the initial success of Martinique and Guadeloupe was followed by a period of distress in the
1670s, as prices and profits fell, and by halting expansion thereafter. For the
French West Indies, as for the British, the great era of colonial trade comes
in the middle of the eighteenth century with the full flowering of the slave
plantation system in Saint Domingue (and Jamaica).

With limited opportunities for plunder, loot, barter, and trade with the
Amerindians, the British in North America turned to settled agriculture
from the first. Eighty to 85 percent of the early colonists earned their living
in agriculture, the majority as outright owners of their farms. They thus fit

Domar's first category:[23] free land combines with free labor; there is little tenancy; there is little or no landlord class. Only New York bore a resemblance to the English situation. For British North America, tenancy is a negligible institution.

Stephen Innes provides an excellent example of tenancy in New England.[24] Of the one-third of adult males in pre-Revolutionary Springfield, Massachusetts, who rented land, only 10 percent had no other source of income. Tenancy was not part of the basic structure of economic organization: it was a way to acquire a freehold and move on, or else an auxiliary status to the tenants' main occupations. In Innes's sample, some tenants moved on, some had middle class occupations; some rented to tide themselves over temporary difficulties; some merely leased animals; some were friends of the landowner and had other holdings.

With no supply of labor forthcoming, no large specialized farms emerged. The colonists turned to mixed farming, based on grain (corn, wheat, barley, oats, and rye), garden vegetables, small orchards, various kinds of livestock, dairy cattle, and sheep. This agriculture was static in nature, with slow technical change, small capital investment, and slow productivity increase, providing no other sources of growth than population increase. Whatever vestiges of communalism or corporatism in colonial mentality and custom survived from the initial era of settlement, the American colonists lived in a market-oriented society. Estimates of the share of output marketed vary widely, from a bare minimum in the near-subsistence economies of the poorest New England soil to as much as 40 percent late in the colonial period on the rich farms of southeast Pennsylvania.

To whom will colonial farmers market their surpluses? For the surpluses cannot be realized without buyers. To acquire manufactures, those commodities they cannot grow, the amenities they do not produce, they must trade. Without capital or technical change, their per capita incomes will grow only by gains from trade. Their economic organization as owner-occupiers puts them in a disadvantageous position: they cannot market to one another, they are too small to risk specialization, they are too diversified to have a staple crop. European capital for such development is not forthcoming: who would set up an agricultural enterprise in a situation where no labor supply can be anticipated?

To say that farmers can market their surpluses in the urban sector merely pushes the question back further: what will be the economic basis of the urban sector? This is a preindustrial world, and there is no significant manufacturing sector in colonial America. How then will cities earn the wherewithal to pay for agricultural commodities? The colonial cities were, of course, port cities, mercantile in function, depending on trade and shipping in the first instance and on linkages and multiplier effects beyond that. What can they trade and to whom? The natural resource base of the American colonies was too slim a reed for economic development. The fur trade dwindled, and neither timber nor fish found a secure, expanding demand in the European market. Only the grain of southeast Pennsylvania succeeded in finding a market in southern Europe, and this trade provides a real exception, for not until the third-quarter of the nineteenth century is American grain able to conquer the European market on a large scale.

Thus, without an organization conducive to large-scale staple production, the road to economic development will be blocked until a market is found for something the colonists can produce. They may live well, better than in Britain, for they pay no rent to a landlord, but without trade or technical change they will simply spread across the landscape as population grows, replicating their mixed farms at the same income levels. And if they decide not to spread across the landscape, they will eventually face lower per capita incomes as population becomes denser and diminishing returns set in.

Development awaits a staple crop which can successfully penetrate European markets, and this is likely to require large-scale specialized farms capable of exploiting economies of scale. And this brings us to the second Domar alternative: free land combined with a landlord class and an unfree labor force.

Slavery and the Founding of American Empires

Two hundred years after Columbus arrived in America, the economic impact of the New World upon the old was hardly felt, as Columbus's vain effort to exploit his discovery was replicated by others. Europeans failed to extract much loot or tribute, to stimulate trade by barter, or to found profitable settlements, and the Western hemisphere remained a negligible trading partner for Europe. In 1692, the first Spanish bullion era was over, and only Virginia in North America, Barbados in the Caribbean, and Brazil in South America were established on firm economic foundations. Building upon these foundations would in each case depend on slavery.

Slavery solved the problem of colonial development by ensuring a supply of labor for potential European investors, enabling them to build up colonies directed to export agriculture, thus setting up a flow of primary products to Europe and a return flow of manufactures to the Western hemisphere. The labor of slaves was elastically supplied, especially productive, and suited to crops with expanding demand. Europeans found profitable investment opportunities which family farms never presented, and large plantation owners could even begin to generate capital themselves.

If we shift our perspective from 1692, to the mid-eighteenth century, the scene changes dramatically. The foreign trade of Europe has turned toward the west, the colonies are developing trade relations with the metropolis, and the Americas have risen to economic and military importance in world politics.

Slavery was the sine qua non of this trade. With slave labor, the British West Indies, led by Jamaica and the Leeward Islands, exported two to three times as much sugar to England and Wales as in 1700.[25] With slave labor, Saint Domingue had even surpassed the British colonies, far outstripping Guadeloupe and Martinique, and had become the most successful colony in the New World. With slave labor, British North America had expanded her tobacco production and was successfully marketing rice, indigo, and cotton in Europe. With slave labor, Cuba would begin to develop a sugar industry whose exports in time would rival all those of New Spain. This rise in colonial exports was matched by a return flow of European exports to the colonies, including Britain's northern colonies, whose export earnings were derived from their earnings in the West Indies. The European centers that produced these exports were the leading sources of industrial growth in their homelands.

Columbus's quest was fulfilled 250 years after he first set foot on land. The coming of slavery had initiated a period of trade and development which benefitted all the participants except those on whose labor the entire structure depended.

Notes

1. K. Sale, *The Conquest of Paradise: Christopher Columbus and the Columbian Legacy*, (New York 1990), 106.

2. Ibid.

3. P. Vilar, *History of Gold and Money*, 1450–1920, (London 1976), 63.

4. D. Watts, *The West Indies: Patterns of Development, Culture, and Environmental Change Since 1492*, (Cambridge, England 1987), 126.

5. For a formal discussion of the proposition that where land is freely available there will never be a supply of voluntary labor to a landlord class, see E. D., Domar, "The Causes of Slavery or Serfdom: A Hypothesis," in: *Journal of Economic History* 30/1 (February 1970) 18–32. I have discussed the applicability of this proposition in *Slavery and Colonization*, in: B. L. Solow (ed.), *Slavery and the Rise of the Atlantic System*, ªCambridge, England and New York 1991), 35–37.

6. Watts, *West Indies* (1987), 78.

7. H. and P. Chaunu, *Seville et l'Atlantique, 1504–1550*, 5 vols., (Paris 1955–56).

8. The paraphrase of the Chaunu argument and the above quotation are taken from J. H. Elliott, *The Old World and the New, 1492–1650*, (Cambridge, England 1970), 68–69.

9. J. H. Parry, *The Spanish Seaborne Empire*, (London 1986), 246–249. The same picture emerges from more modern sources. Cf. Watts, *West Indies* (1987), Fig. 4.1, 130.

10. H. Kamen, *Spain 1469–1714: A Society of Conflict*, (London 1983).

11. P. Bakewell, "Mining," in: L. Bethel' (ed.), *Colonial Spanish America*, (Cambridge, England 1987), 03–249.

12. Bakewell, "Mining" (1987), 229–230.

13. Bakewell, "Mining" (1987), chart 3A, 237.

14. C. P., Kindleberger, *Spenders and Hoarders: The World Distribution of Spanish Silver, 1550–1750*, in his Historical Economics: Art or Science? (Berkeley 1990), 46.

15. Kindleberger, *Spenders* (1990), 44.

16. Ibid., 112.

17. Ibid., 49.

18. Ibid., 42–43, citing Altman and Wilson.

19. D. A. Brading, 149.

20. S. B. Schwartz, *Sugar Plantations in the Formation of Brazilian Society: Bahia, 1550–1835*, (Cambridge, England 1985), reprinted 1989.

21. C. and R. Bridenbaugh, *No Peace Beyond the Line: The English in the Caribbean, 1624–1690*, (New York 1972), 23–24.

22. For the dating of the transition from free to slave labor in the British West Indies, see B. L. Solow, "The Transition from Free Labor to Slavery in the British West Indies," in: *De la Traite a l'Escalavages, Actes du Collogue International sur la Traite des Noirs*, (Paris 1989), Vol. 1, 89–110.

23. Domar, Causes (cf. note 5).

24. S. Innes, *Labor in a New Land: Economy and Society in Seventeenth Century Springfield*, (Princeton, NJ 1983).

25. R.B. Sheriden, *Sugar and Slavery: An Economic History of the West Indies, 1623–1775*, (Baltimore 1970), 487–88.

CHAPTER FIVE

~

Caribbean Slavery and British Growth*

The paper supports the hypothesis advanced by Eric Williams that slavery in the British West Indies contributed significantly to English industrial growth in the second half of the eighteenth century. Objections are raised to earlier criticisms of the Williams hypothesis, and a simple Cobb-Douglas model is used to demonstrate how the slave colonies contributed to home country growth, and that this contribution was quantitatively important. The paper concludes that colonial slavery increased British national income and the pool: of investable funds and resulted in a pattern of trade that encouraged industrialization.

In his valuable survey of Caribbean historiography, Green (1977) reminds us that scholarly work for the last three decades has centered around one author and one book, Green writes: "Since the publication of Capitalism and Slavery, historical writing on the British West Indies has, to a large extent, involved a conscious confirmation or refutation of (Eric) Williams" several theses.[1] The attack on Williams's work was begun by Anstey (1968). Papers by Thomas (1968) and Coelho (1973), though not specifically directed at his work, were thought to have damaged his thesis irreparably. Engerman (1972, 1975) has continued the criticism, and most recently Drescher (1977) has vigorously attacked his book.[2]

*I would like to thank my sons, Andrew R. and John L. Solow, for assistance in producing the mathematical results, and my husband, Robert M. Solow, for assistance in producing the sons.

These criticisms have been directed at very different aspects of Williams's work, and there is no unanimity among the critics. For example, some argue that *Capitalism and Slavery* overestimates the contribution of the British West Indies to British economic development, while others argue that the colonies were a source of significant and undiminished profitability until the era of abolition. In this state of affairs, it is clear that the last word on the Williams thesis has not been spoken.

It is even possible that Williams's case for the importance of the connection between slavery and European expansion goes beyond his English example. The perception of this connection revolutionizes what every schoolboy thinks he knows about European expansion. A fair summary of the conventional wisdom would be illustrated by the following quotation from an eminent authority:[3]

"The westward expansion of Europe after 1492, rested on the foundation of eighty years of Portuguese enterprise in the Atlantic. Portugal was the Atlantic pioneer, colonizing Atlantic islands and exploring and trading down the west coast of Africa. It was in Portugal that a body of ocean sailing and navigation was built up during the fifteenth century, and it was almost accidental that at the climax of Portuguese pioneering enterprise the most crucial of all the discoveries was made by a Genoese in the service of Spain."

In fact the westward expansion of Europe after 1492, rested on the foundation of the expansion of Europe from the time of the First Crusade, primarily by Italians from Venice and Genoa. The economic aspect of this expansion comprised both commercial and productive activity; the productive activity was primarily though not exclusively in sugar plantations; the sugar plantations were organized with slave labor.[4] There was nothing accidental in the Genoese origin of Columbus, whose father-in-law owned a sugar plantation.

European expansion exhibits a continuity which begins in the Holy Land, Crete, Cyprus, then continues to the Canaries, Madeira, and .the Azores, and the islands off the African Coast, before crossing to the New World. Once this is grasped, the association of sugar and slavery with European expansion becomes clearer, for it is with sugar and slaves that Europeans hop-scotched from island to island in the course of this expansion.

An effort to link slavery with European growth has been made by William A. Darity,[5] using a three-sector general equilibrium international trade model involving Europe, Africa, and the American colonies to test the validity of what he calls the Caribbean School. This he takes as comprising the work of Williams, Walter Rodney, and C.L.R. James, and the propositions he tests growth include not only Williams's contention that the triangular trade helped develop Europe, but also that it resulted in falling colonial and African incomes.

Darity's model includes two effects due to Rodney, that the trade constitutes a learning curve for European technology and a retrogression in Africa (due to depopulation and social disruption). With plausible parameters, the model is shown to be consistent with the predictions of the Caribbean School. The Darity model reaches broader conclusions than the present article and makes some different assumptions, but there is substantial agreement in some of our views.[6]

Part of the difficulty in dealing with *Capitalism and Slavery* arises because it is not precisely clear what the Williams thesis is, and therefore it is difficult to frame a test that will accept or reject it. In the broadest terms, Williams is relating something about slavery to something that is happening in Great Britain. The "something about slavery" appears, in different parts of the book, to be the profits of the slave trade, or the entire triangular trade, or the value of the British West Indies, or the commercial policy embodied in the Navigation Acts. The "something in Great Britain" appears variously as economic growth, or the Industrial Revolution, or mature capitalism, or even free trade. In the one place it is "slavery (as) an economic institution" which "produced the cotton to serve as a base for modern capitalism" (p. 5). In another place it is the profits from the triangular trade which "provided one of the main streams of that accumulation of capital in England which financed the Industrial Revolution" (p. 52). And what are we to make of this: "But it must not be inferred that the triangular trade was solely and entirely responsible for the economic development. The growth of the internal market in England, the ploughing-in of the profits from industry to generate still further capital and achieve still greater expansion, played a large part. But this industrial development, stimulated by mercantilism later outgrew mercantilism and destroyed it." And this: "The rise and fall of mercantilism is the rise and fall of slavery" (p. 136). Thus critics can hardly be blamed for "erecting straw men." There are plenty of them in the book. But a careful reading will, I think, reveal a logical and comprehensive argument.

After all, it took a generation of economists to elucidate "what Keynes really meant," and Williams was not Keynes.

The Williams Hypothesis

What did Williams "really mean"? I shall argue that, properly understood, *Capitalism and Slavery* constituted a new and original reading of West Indian and British history. It was no mere restatement of Mercantilist fallacies; it demolished racial origin theories of slavery; it cast serious doubts upon the conventional interpretation of the anti-slavery movement. Indeed, *Capitalism and Slavery* deserved Henry Steele Commager's praise on the cover as ". . . one of the most learned, most penetrating and most significant (books) that has appeared in this field of history".

To get an idea of Williams's achievement, recall the views that held the field when *Capitalism and Slavery* appeared in 1944. The argument that the British West Indies had been of great economic value to England, a position advanced by Mercantilist authors and by spokesmen for the West Indian planting interests, had been killed by the authority of Adam Smith: "Under the present system of management, therefore, Great Britain derives nothing but loss from the dominion which she assumes over her colonies."[7] The colonial empire of which the British West Indies were a part was believed to have been an unfortunate episode of economic drain on the mother country, erroneously thought beneficial by contemporaries because they did not understand the consequences of misallocation of resources due to a policy of economic monopoly. The presence of slaves in the British West Indies played no role in this assessment, and the economic analysis of slavery in the English and American literature in 1944, was conspicuous by its absence. Almost a century of silence separates the end of the Wakefield-Merivale-Cairnes tradition from Conrad and Meyer. Instead the presence of slave economies in the West Indies was accounted for by theories of race and climate, by the social class background of the white settlers, or merely not explained at all. The abolition of the slave trade was viewed as a triumph of Enlightenment ideology, pushed through by a tenacious and effective propaganda effort. In this setting, *Capitalism and Slavery* offered a new and original view of the economic link between the islands and the mother country, a different (not wholly new) view of the origin of western hemisphere slavery, and a new view of the politics of abolition, emancipation, and the equalization of sugar duties.

In this paper I shall try to clarify Williams's argument relating the slave economies of the British West Indies to economic growth in Great Britain in the eighteenth century, to show that his argument remains unaffected by the criticisms which have been directed against it, and I shall introduce a simple model which will enable me to demonstrate that the magnitudes involved were significant. Finally, I shall argue that the result is compatible with what we know of British economic growth in the eighteenth century from modern data.

For Williams, the institution of black slavery in the Americas was economic in origin, not racial. For economic reasons, the growing of certain crops was associated with coerced labor, first white and Amerindian, later black African. Racism is the result of slavery, not the cause: the consequence of a status whose origin was economic in nature. Without coerced black labor, the settlers of the Caribbean colonies were struggling in a losing battle to raise inferior crops of tobacco, indigo and cotton. Before slavery there was (and without slavery there would have been) a trickle of trade between the colonies and the mother country. The exchange of West Indian sugar for British manufactures could not have taken place at the levels actually achieved without the institution of slavery. The external trade of the North American colonies also depended to a considerable extent on the Caribbean slave colonies, for only by the surpluses earned in those colonies could the North Americans cover their deficit with the home country. The magnitude, content, and pattern of international trade would have been quite different and less favorable for Great Britain at an important stage of her economic development had emigration from Africa, like emigration from Europe, been voluntary.

This is the first step in Williams's argument. The capital expended in the West Indies could have been expended elsewhere (for example, at home), but would have received a lower rate of return. This increase was an important source of new investment for England. The higher rate of return in the colonies was due to the existence of an elastic supply of a particularly cheap form of labor. Before slaves were available, the land in the colonies was less valuable and the return on capital lower. Indeed, at an early date colonial enterprises were barely profitable, land nearly valueless, and the return on capital perhaps even below that at home. Once slavery came, land was valued and utilized profitably; total product in the Empire was larger; total trade increased and the opportunities for division of labor increased as well.

The linking of the profitability of the colonies with slavery is an original and important insight attributed to Williams. Moreover, other arguments linking the colonies with economic growth at home had measured their contribution by return on capital invested (Sheridan) or by share of trade (Drescher) or by post hoc propter hoc arguments (Boulle and Richardson).[8] All of these arguments for the importance of the colonies to metropolitan growth deduce significance from size. They are all vulnerable to the simple economic observation that significance must be measured by the opportunity cost of the factors involved. The value of the colonies to Great Britain can only be established by comparing the returns on the capital invested there with the returns on the next best alternative. Williams's formulation addresses the counterfactual situation directly and does not make the simple error of the others.

Criticisms by Engerman and Thomas

The principal arguments against the Williams hypothesis have been, first, that the quantitative importance of the West Indies was simply too small to matter to British growth, and second, that, properly measured, the colonies were a net loss, not a gain to the Empire. I shall argue that neither of these criticisms is valid.

An attempt to evaluate Williams's claim for the link between slavery and British growth was made by Engerman (1972). His method was to estimate the profits of the slave trade for a series of years and see what proportion they bore to (1) British national income, (2) British total domestic investment, (3) commercial and industrial investment. Secondly, recognizing that "a fair reading of Williams would indicate that he . . . would emphasize (not) solely . . . the slave trade (but) rather the entire plantation economy system," Engerman added to the profits of the slave trade an estimate of the value of the profits on British West Indian trade to the home economy and calculated the ratio of this wider measure to the various British magnitudes mentioned above.

Engerman's technique was to overstate the possible contribution by biasing upward his profit estimates and by biasing upward their flow into investment. An example of this is the assumption that all profits were invested at home and none were retained in the colony or reinvested in the slave trade or devoted to consumption. He thus sought to derive an upper limit on what the West Indian contribution could have been. If this turned out to be small, in his view the Williams case—at least in that version—could be rejected. The conclusion Engerman reached is best stated in his own careful words (pp. 441–42):

> These exercises . . . are meant only to show that, even under some implausible assumptions, the aggregate contribution of slave trade profits to the financing of British capital formation in the eighteenth century could not be so large as to bear weight as the, or a, major contributing factor . . .
>
> "The contribution of the profits from the slave trade plus those estimated by Sheridan from the West Indian plantations was below five per cent of British income in an early year in the Industrial Revolution. . . . It is rather clear that a basically static neo-classical model cannot provide a favorable outcome for arguments such as those of Eric Williams."

I shall argue that Engerman's conclusions do not follow from his own statistical work, in other words, that the proportion of slave trade profits to capital formation is not insignificant for the period of the beginning of accelerated British growth, and that the ratio of the sum of slave trade profits plus total profits on West Indian investment to British capital formation, again as estimated by Engerman, is so large as to be quite incredible. My contention is not of course that this establishes Williams's case, only that it is inadmissible to dismiss it on the grounds Engerman advances.

According to Engerman's estimates, the ratio of slave trade profits to national income in Great Britain ranges from 0.0012 to 0.0054, the peak year being 1770. The ratio of such profits to capital formation ranges from a low of 2.4 percent to a high of 10.8 percent. Actually, the 10.8 percent is an overestimate, because Engerman's denominator (investment) for the peak year is artificially low. Investment is calculated at 5 percent of national income by Engerman, on the basis of Deane and Cole's estimate that it rose from 3 percent early in the century to 7 percent at the end. A linear interpolation would accordingly lower the ratio of slave trade profits to investment at the end of the period and raise it at the beginning (compared with Engerman's figures). I have adjusted the ratio accordingly. Next, Engerman accepts Deane and Cole's rough guess that commercial and industrial investment constituted 20 percent of total investment at the end of the eighteenth century from less than 10 percent at the beginning. This forms the basis of calculating slave trade profits in relation to commercial and industrial investment.

Table 5.1 summarizes the results of these comparisons. Focusing on 1770, the closest date we have for relating the colonies' contribution to the accelerated growth of the eighteenth century, we find that the overstated slave trade profits form one half of 1 percent of national income, nearly eight percent of total investment, and 31 percent of commercial and industrial investment.

These ratios are not small; they are enormous. The ratio of *total* corporate profits of domestic industries to GNP in the United States today (1980) amounts to 6 percent. The ratio of total corporate domestic profits to gross private domestic investment for that year amounts to over 40 percent. And the ratio of total corporate domestic profits to 1980, investment in domestic plant and equipment (non-residential fixed investment) runs at more than 55 percent. These figures come from *Economic Indicators* (September 1981).

How can we be sure the ratio of slave trade profits to national income in 1770 is "small" at half a percent, when the ratio of total corporate profits to GNP today is only 6 percent? If slave trade profits were 8 percent of investment in Britain in 1770, is that "small" when today total corporate profits amount to 40 percent? No industry manages as much as 8 percent. Is the

Table 5.1. Slave trade profits as percent of national income; investment, and commercial and industrial investment.[a]

	Slave trade profits (£ mil)	National income (£ mil)	Investment (£ mil)	Comm./Ind. Investment (£ mil)	Slave trade profits as a % of		
					National income	Investment	Comm./Ind. Investment
1688	0.179	48.0	1.4	0.14	0.37	13	128.[b]
1710	0.110	57.4	2.3	0.28	0.19	4.7	39.3
1730	0.056	46.6	2.3	0.35	0.12	2.4	16.0
1750	0.215	51.7	3.1	0.54	0.42	6.9	39.8
1770	0.342	62.8	4.4	0.88	0.54	7.8	38.9

[a]Source: Engerman (1972) and text.

[b]No significance is to be attributed to this figure beyond the demonstration that commercial and industrial investment in 1688 was very small in a year of large slave trade profits; the number cannot be taken seriously.

potential contribution of an industry whose profits can "only" amount to 39 percent of commercial and industrial investment to be ruled out because it is "small"?

Naturally it is not my intention to make a serious comparison between 1770 and 1980, nor to claim that these figures make a case for Williams. Engerman never claims that they measure anything but an upper limit on what the slave trade could have contributed to British growth. On the evidence of his figures, the contribution *could have been* enormous. There is no basis in this statistical exercise for overruling Williams's view.

But it was Williams's contention that it was not just the profits of the slave trade but the profits of the entire plantation economy in the West Indies that gave the impetus to British growth. To test this wider hypothesis, Engerman added Sheridan's estimate—admittedly a contested figure—of the contribution of the West Indies profits to the home economy for 1770 (£2,578,300) to the slave trade profits; the resulting figure amounted to something under 5 percent of British national income, or an amount very close to Britain's entire gross domestic investment. Whether, with Sheridan's figure, the colonial contribution amounts to 2 percent of Arthur Young's national income estimate for 1770, or 4 percent of the national income generated from Deane and Cole, the crucial thing to keep in mind is that total gross domestic investment amounted to less than 7 percent of national income, reaching that level only at the end of the century.

If Sheridan's figure is wrong by a factor of two then that would hardly alter the conclusion: there is no basis for rejecting the Williams thesis. There is no basis for accepting it either; but we cannot rule out the contention that the profits of the slave trade and those derived from the West Indian colonies were quantitatively large compared with total British investment and with commercial and industrial investment, at the beginning of the Industrial Revolution. The naive view that the sheer size of income derived from the West Indian colonies constitutes the measure of their contribution to British growth—a view of which Williams must be acquitted—was argued by Sheridan (1965) and criticized by Thomas (1968). By recalculating some of Sheridan's numbers and adopting a different method of measuring the colonies' contribution, Thomas concluded (p. 38): "For the year 1773 the income of Englishmen would have been at least £631,750 higher had the West Indies not been a part of the empire." It appears from the preceding that Adam Smith was correct, at least with respect to the sugar colonies—they were "mere loss instead of profit".

In fact, Thomas's refutation of Sheridan was basically Adam Smith's reply to supporters of the West Indian colonies. Thomas writes (p. 31): "The contribution of a colony of any economic activity to the economic growth of the overall economy is precisely the difference (positive or negative) earned by the resources employed there relative to what they would have earned in their next best alternative." Second, the private rate of return is not necessarily the correct measure of the colony's contribution, since it may differ from the social rate of return. In this particular case, Smith and Thomas argue, the tariff preference granted the colonies inflicted on the mother country the cost of buying expensive sugar from British colonies instead of cheap sugar elsewhere. This cost must be deducted from the private rate of return. And the military and administrative costs of the colonies ought to be deducted as well.

To arrive at his numerical conclusion, Thomas estimated the value of the capital stock in the colonies (including slaves) at £37 million for 1773. He assumed that this capital invested at home would not have yielded a lower rate of return—in other words, that the marginal efficiency of capital schedule was not downward sloping—because the investment in the West Indies was small relative to total capital investment at home. Biasing the case for a positive contribution of the colonies, Thomas assumed the £37 million would have earned a return of 3.5 percent (the consol rate in 1773) at home. This amounts to £1,295,000. The income actually generated in the colonies that year he estimated at £1,450,750. From this Thomas deducted the loss on account of tariff protection in sugar (£383,000) and the cost of naval and military protection of the islands (£379,000). Subtracting these offsets from the income earned resulted in a social return from the colonies of only £688,500 or at least £606,500 *less* than English income would have been without the colonies. If Thomas's numbers are approximately correct and if his method is correct, the Williams hypothesis would fail.[9]

The reply of *Capitalism and Slavery* to this argument would be that in the absence of the West Indies the £37 million invested at home would have driven down the rate of interest. Williams offered as evidence a collection of miscellaneous quotes from English eighteenth century economists (p. 52). Sir Josiah Child estimated that one white and ten blacks would bring employment for four men in England. Davenant said that one Englishman in the West Indies, with slaves, brought in as much profit as seven men in England. Another author asserted that every British West Indian family brought in twenty times the profit they would have made at home. And so on. The sense of these remarks is that Williams believed that investment at home was subject to diminishing returns, but not in the colonies, on account of slavery. Capital invested in the colonies was earning a profit (and would continue to earn a profit) that was unmatched by extra-marginal domestic opportunities.

What Thomas has measured is not the gain to Britain in the absence of the West Indies, but an estimate of the consequences of a tariff against French sugar and of maintaining a colonial administration and naval forces there. It is the particular commercial and imperial policies he has addressed, not the value of the West Indies.[10]

The framework of the discussion goes back to the classical economists and the familiar idea that (in the kind of economy they posited), profits would fall, the diminishing returns to capital being due to the fixity of land. This would lead to the classical stationary state. But, as Ricardo said [Sraffa (1951, p. 179)], "If with every accumulation of capital we could tack a piece of fertile land to our Island, profits would never fall." Ricardo envisaged eventual falling profits at home and expected that capital would be exported to countries not yet at England's stage. He foresaw two kinds of gains from trade: from specialization and division of labor on the one hand, and from higher returns to capital on the other.

Adam Smith also saw the acquisition of new territory as a source of an increased rate of profit (p. 93): "For some time after the conclusion of the late war, not only private people of the best credit, but some of the greatest companies in London, commonly borrowed at 5 percent, who before that had been used to pay not more than 4, and 4½ percent. The great accession both of territory and trade, by our acquisitions in North America and the West Indies, will sufficiently account for this, without supposing any diminution in the capital stock of the society."

It was Wakefield who pointed out that the addition of free land would not raise profits because in simple agricultural economies there will be no supply of labor to landowners and, the capital needs of yeomen being small, a person with capital to invest has no source of labor to accompany his investment. Coerced labor solves this problem; where there is slavery, capital can flow; and free land will then indeed be associated with counteracting the fall in the marginal product of capital.

This simple model accords with the historical fact that after the New World was discovered, the flow of trade and capital was disproportionately directed toward slave economies: Brazil, the Caribbean, and the Chesapeake and Virginia. What moved in international trade was to a large extent slave-grown crops and plantation-connected goods.[11]

If British national income were £130 million in 1770, as Deane and Cole suggest, and the capital/output ratio was two to one, the capital invested in the colonies amounted to 14 percent of that invested at home.[12] There is ample reason then to assume that had the capital been invested at home it would have been subject to diminishing marginal returns. Williams's argument is that diminishing returns to investment in the colony were held at bay by the easy availability of slave labor. For every pound invested in every acre marked out for cane, there was an ample flow of labor available; it was "the one needful thing", as Georgians were to express it later on, for profitable investing.

I conclude then that the Williams hypothesis has neither been disproved because the magnitudes are too small, as Engerman argued, nor because the colonies can be shown to be a net loss to England, as Thomas argued. The Williams hypothesis can be illustrated in simple terms and shown to result in plausibly significant effects on British economic growth.

Model of Williams Hypothesis

We want to compare the profits on a certain amount of capital invested at home and in a colony. Using a Cobb-Douglas production function, $Y - Aka$ where output Y is a function of capital K and all other factors A, which are fixed, we can draw the relationship between capital K and the return on capital r; it will be of constant elasticity $-(1-x)$ from the Cobb-Douglas assumption.

Suppose an amount of capital $K0$ is invested with rate of return $r0$. Then let a proportionately greater amount of capital $xK0$ be invested under conditions of diminishing returns (home) or constant returns (colony), and see what the ratio of the profits in the former case is to profits in the latter case of figure 5.1.

In the colony an investment of $(1 + x)K0$ at $r0$ results in profits described by the rectangle $0r0B[(1 + x)K0]$. The gain over the initial investment of K is the rectangle $K0AB[(1 + x)K0]$ or $r0xK0$.

At home, the profits from \an investment of $(1 + x)K0$ are described by the rectangle $0r1C[(1 + x)K0]$ or $r1(1 + x)K0$. The gain from the additional capital is the difference between the two rectangles $K0DC(1+x)K0 - r1r0AD$, or $r1xK0 - (r0-r1)K0$.

We seek the ratio between the two respective returns to the additional investment,

$$\frac{r0xK0}{r1xK0 - (r0 - r1)K0} = \frac{r0x}{r1x - r0 + r1}$$

$$\frac{x}{(r1/r0)x + (r\ dr0) - 1} = \frac{x}{(r1/r0)(1 + x) - 1}$$

With constant elasticity of $-(1 - x)$,

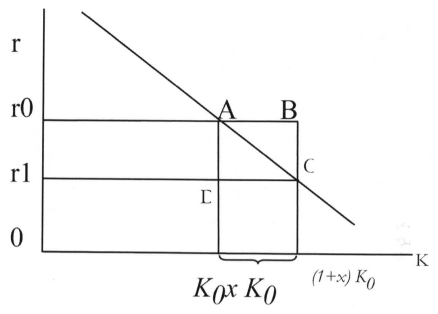

Figure 5.1.

$$\frac{\Delta r}{r} = -(1-x)\,\frac{\Delta K}{K}, \quad \frac{\Delta r}{r} = \frac{r1-r0}{r0} = -(1-x)\,x,$$

$$\frac{r1}{r0} = -(1-x)\,x, \quad \frac{r1}{r0} = 1-(1-x)\,x.$$

Then,

$$\frac{x}{(r1/r0)(1+x)-1} = \frac{x}{[1-(1-a)x](1+x)-1}$$

If $a = \frac{1}{4}$, a usual assumption for the coefficient, and x is very small, the profit on that pound of capital invested in the colony is four times greater than the profit on that pound invested at home. If x is as large as 15 percent, which it might very well be, the ratio of profit on colonial compared with home investment becomes

$$\frac{1}{\frac{1}{4} - (\frac{3}{4} \times 0.15)} \quad \text{or about 7.}$$

Thus, with plausible numbers, £37 million invested in the British West Indies returned a profit of four to seven times greater than the alternative investment opportunity at home. If the £37 million returned £1.48 in the colony, less than £250,000 would have been returned at home. If total investment at home ran at 6 percent of a national income of £130 million, the difference due to the greater profits in the colonies would have been substantial. It could have amounted to 12 or 14 percent of total British investment.

Thus the additional profits on capital generated by slave labor in the British West Indies were a source of a significant amount of saving, which found its way into investing in the industrial sector of the home country. There are two steps to the argument. Had the capital invested in the colonies been retained at home, aggregate profits would have been lower by the amount $(r0-r1)(1+x)K0$ as shown in Fig. 1. (Moreover, as is shown in the appendix, to the extent that free labor in England was dearer than slave labor in the colonies, the loss associated with investing the capital at home would have been greater still.)

Aggregate income in Britain would have been lower only by the amount represented by the triangle ABC. The difference represents the fact that other factors of production at home—land and labor—would have gained an amount of income $r0ACr1$ by virtue of higher capital/land and capital/labor ratios generated by the extra home investment. But wages and rents in preindustrial society are considered to have been spent on subsistence and conspicuous consumption; profits were the main source of saving.[13]

The second step in the argument depends on the fact that the colonies exported sugar and imported manufactures. The particular commodity composition of the trade helped direct the extra saving into industrial activity: it was slave labor that ultimately permitted British manufactures to be traded for Caribbean sugar (and permitted North Americans to earn sterling with which to import those same manufactures).

Implications for British Growth

The argument Williams advanced in *Capitalism and Slavery* is compatible with Deane and Cole's account of the early stages of British industrialization and with the data underlying that account. In explaining the accelerated growth of England and Wales in the last two decades of the eighteenth century, they think it is a reasonable assumption that over a fifth of national income rose in sympathy with the soaring volume of domestic exports (p. 281). Major export industries had a higher growth rate than most others. By the end of the eighteenth century, domestic exports of England and Wales in relation to national income were double their ratio of a century before (p.

309). Even more significant, Deane and Cole found it probable that in the eighteenth century about a third of industrial output was exported (p. 312). They conclude that "the existence of exploitable international markets at the end of the eighteenth and beginning of the nineteenth centuries was probably crucial in initiating the process of industrialization and the growth in real incomes which was associated with it" (p. 312). The case for export-led growth they think is strong.

This trade expansion of the eighteenth century, as is well known, was associated with the colonial trade. European governments were protection-ist, and potential expansion in continental markets was thwarted. Europe's share in British trade declined from about 82 percent of domestic exports and 62 percent of all imports in 1700–01, to about 21 percent of exports and 29 percent of imports in 1797–98. Although this is exaggerated by wartime conditions at the latter date, it reflects a true shift on a massive scale: British exports to America rose twenty fold over the eighteenth century (p. 86). "It was the American market (including the valuable West Indies) which provided the greatest scope for growth" (p. 34). According to Deane and Cole's figures, the British West Indies took 10 percent of British domestic exports in 1700–01, 37 percent in 1772–73, and 57 percent in the disturbed conditions of 1797–98. The corresponding figures for imports plus reexports are 20 percent, 36 percent, and 31 percent. Dean and Cole were hesitant to ascribe an exogenous role to the colonies—observing that colonial demand for British exports is dependent on British purchases of colonial goods—but the arguments of Williams provide the missing link which enables us to ascribe to the slaves in the British West Indies an independent role in the economic growth and industrialization of eighteenth century Britain. Slavery made more profits for investment, a larger national income for the Empire, and a pattern of trade which strengthened the comparative advantage of the home country in industrial commodities. A proper appreciation of Williams's powerful and original insight is long overdue. Something perhaps is also due to the slaves of the British West Indies, of whom it ought not be said that they toiled from sunup to sundown in the cane fields without conferring any economic advantages on those who enslaved them.

Appendix

The same result (with minor differences) can be derived more directly. Let the income in the Home Country (Y) be a function of the capital (K) invested there, and all other factors (A), where A includes the effect of all other factors, such as labor.

$Y = AK^x$.

The total return to capital in the Home Country will be

(1) $$_xAK^x.$$

Suppose there is a colony where an amount OK is invested at the same rate of return. There are no diminishing returns to investment in the colony because the appropriate number of units of labor can be added with every unit of land. The aggregate profit of investment of OK in the colony is

(2) $$OKxAKa^{x-1} \text{ or } OxAK^x.$$

Suppose now that the additional 0K had been invested instead at home.

Total profit would be

(3) $$xA(1+O) \, ^xK^x.$$

The difference between (1) and (3) is given by

$xAk^x[(1 + O) \, x - 1]$ or approximately $xAK^x(x0)$,

and what is added in the colony is $1/x$ times what is added at home.

If we take a $x = ¼$, a usual assumption for modern economies, the real return on the investment in the colonies is four times what would be obtained by investing it at home. In any case, x is a fraction, and whatever its value, there will be a multiplied return to colonial investment.

There will be another source of additional return associated with colonial investment if the full cost of a unit of slave labor (maintenance plus capital cost) is below the wage of a free laborer at home.

From a Cobb-Douglas function with constant returns to scale, we can drive the factor price frontier, which will relate the return to capital to the wage. This is given by

(4) $$r = \left(\frac{w}{(1-x)A} \right)^{(x-1)a} xA.$$

The return of investing OK in the colony is

(5)
$$r_b OK_a,$$

where rb is the rate of profit in the colony. The additional return on an investment of OK at home—the difference between investing $(1+0)K$ and K is given by

$$(r_a (1 + 0)^x - 1)K_a \text{ or approximately } x0r_a K_a.$$

Thus, the ratio of the return in the colony to the added return at home is

$$\frac{RbOKa}{X0ra - Ka} = \frac{1rb}{xra}$$

From eq. (4) we can express the rs in terms of the free Home Country labor's wage and the colony's slave labor cost. We find that

$rb = \text{constant} \bullet wb^{(x-1)/a}$,
$ra = \text{constant} \bullet wb^{(x-1)/a}$.

Now if $wa = wb$, this reduces to the earlier result, where returns to the colony were $1/x$ of returns at home. But if $wa > wb$, then $1/x$ is multiplied by a number larger than one, and if $x = \frac{1}{4}$ and labor cost is 10 percent higher at home, then profit in the colony is

$$\left(\frac{1}{x}\right)^{(x-1)/a} = \left(\frac{wb}{wa}\right)^{-3} \frac{1}{1.1}$$

or 1.331 x 4=5.324 times that at home.

Notes

1. Williams (1966), Green (1977).
2. See Anstey (1968), Thomas (1968), Coehlho (1973), Engerman (1972, 1975), and Drescher (1977).
3. Davis (1973).
4. A convenient source for the history of European colonization is Verlinden (1970). The most important essays are chapter 1: "The Transfer of Colonial Tech-

niques from the Mediterranean to the Atlantic": chapter 2, "Europe and Colonial Slavery in America"; chapter 4. "Some Aspects of Slavery. in Medieval Italian Colonies"; chapter 6, "Italian Influence on Spaniel: Economy and Colonization during the Reign of Ferdinand the Catholic"; and chapter 7, "the Italians in the Economy of the Canary Islands at the Beginning of Spanish Colonization."

5. Darity (1982a, pp. 287–326).

6. See especially his footnotes 7, 8 and 14 in which his criticisms of the critics of Williams (Anstey, Engerman and Thomas) partly agree with my own below; and his footnote 11, which argues that Williams's hypothesis fits well with the pattern of British economic growth shown by the Deane and Cole data. In two further papers; he has continued to give support to the Williams thesis. In Darity (1982b, pp. 145–150) he argues for the importance of coerced labor for Jamaica, and stresses that "the hunger for labor from Africa in the nascent stages of the history of capitalism only could be satisfied by the mechanisms of slavery" (p. 149). In Darity (1981, pp. 1–21) he abandons his general equilibrium model in favor of Marxist methodology. In this article he gives Mercantilism a role in a Marxian primitive accumulation that differs from my own understanding; and the essential difference between wage labor and slave labor is not clearly elaborated. Nevertheless, the article is full of interest and bears directly on the important aspects of *Capitalism and Slavery*, many of which are, however, outside the scope of the present paper.

7. Smith (1937, p. 581).

8. See Sheridan (1965), Drescher (1977), Boulle (1975), and Richardson (1975).

9. Thomas's argument is crystal-clear, but there are some problems with his arithmetic. He gives two different figures for the hypothetical rate of return in Great Britain (£1,295,000 on p. 34 and £1,292,500 on p. 38; of which the former is indeed the return on £37 million invested at a consol rate of 3.5). Next; he specifies social costs of £382,250 from buying British, not French sugar and naval costs of £413,000, partially offset by £34,000 in certain revenues from the islands (p. 38). The social cost thus calculated amounts to £762,250. But Thomas refers to a figure of "more than £784,000" (p. 38). This £784,000 he subtracts from the income earned in the colonies of £1,450,750 and gets £660,750 (I get £666,750), which he then subtracts from the (erroneous) £1,292,500.

10. The quantitative estimates that Thomas gives for the cost of foregoing French sugar and of administering and defending the British colonies have been disputed by Sheridan and should not be accepted uncritically. See Sheridan (1968, pp. 57–58).

11. There is no need to limit the association of slavery and British industrial growth to the West Indies. Jacob Price has shown that British capital invested in the North American colonies was concentrated in the tobacco-growing slave states of Maryland and Virginia. His researches have elucidated the link between English credit, tobacco exports; and colonial imports of British goods. In another example, J.V. Beckett has shown how Whitehaven merchants turned from domestic to Atlantic trade with the rise of tobacco in the mid-eighteenth century, and how Sir John Lowther made an effort to establish textile manufactures to provide an export com-

modity for the new trade. Tobacco merchants invested in iron works, glass works, rope walks, shipbuilding, etc. The expansion of Cumbrian cloth centers, which may be ascribed to the same cause, came to little as the tobacco trade moved to Glasgow. But then the link between tobacco and Scottish industrial development has been often argued.

12. Deane and Cole (1967, p. 156). This is reproducible capital (excluding land); a capital–output ratio of 3.2 is given as a guess for 1832 (p. 304), so I chose 2.0 for 1770 quite arbitrarily. It may well be too low. Such estimates are of course only illustrative and not to be taken literally. I have used Deane and Cole's data rather than Feinstein's more recent capital and investment figures (C.H. Feinstein, "Capital Formation in Great Britain," in "Cambridge Economic History of Europe"; Vol. VII), since these figures are related to Deane and Cole estimates of other magnitudes. It seemed inconsistent to inject Feinstein's series into the body of the Deane and Cole data. In any case, all such estimates rely on, in Feinstein's words, "especially before 1800 . . . fragments of evidence glued together with rough guesses and more or less arbitrary assumptions" [Feinstein (1981, p. 129)].

13. Williams believed that the West Indian landlords did the saving and investing; in my version the saving is done from the profits of the West Indian plantations and the investing by the marginal investors in England. It could be argued that the added return due to slavery would have been (in a text-book world) eventually engrossed by the landlords through a bidding up of the price of the fixed factor. This has been pointed out by Thomas (1968, p. 33, fn. 2). In this case; the measure of the increased income and growth in the Empire would be in the increase of land values in the colonies after slavery. In fact, plantation owners would not have distinguished whether their income was due to ownership of land or of reproducible capital.

References

Anstey, Roger T., 1968, Capitalism and slavery: A critique, Economic History Review, 2nd series, 21.

Boulle, Pierre, 1975, "Marchandises de traite et développement industriel dans la France et l'Angleterre de XVIIIe siècle," Revue française d'histoire d'outre-mer 62.

Coelho, Philip R.P., 1973, "The profitability of imperialism: The British experience in the West Indies, 1768-1772," Explorations in Economic History, 10.

Darity, William A., Jr., 1981, Mercantilism, slavery and the Industrial Revolution, Research in Political Economy 5.

Darity, William A., J.; 1982a, "A general equilibrium model of the eighteenth-century slave trade: A least-likely test for the Caribbean School" in: Paul Uselding, ed., Research in Ecoconomic History, Vol. 7.

Darity, William A., Jr., 1982b, "The end of the slave trade and indentured immigration, Canadian Journal of African Studies.

Davis, Ralph, 1973, The rise of the Atlantic economies (Cornell University Press, Ithaca, NY).

Deane, Phyllis and W.A. Cole, 1967, British economic growth; 1688–1959: Trends and structure, 2nd ed. (Cambridge University Press, Cambridge).

Drescher, Seymour, 1977, Econocide, British slavery in the era of abolution (University of Pittsburgh Press, Pittsburgh, PA).

Engerman, Stanley L., 1972, "The slave trade and British capital formation in the eighteenth century: A comment on the Williams thesis"; Business History Review 46.

Engerman, Stanley L., 1975, Comments on Richardson and Boulle and the "Williams thesis", Revue française d'histoire d'outre-mer 62.

Feinstein, C.H., 1981, "Capital accumulation and the industrial revolution," in: Roderick Floud and Donald McCloskey; eds., The economic history of Britain since 1700, Vol. 1, 1700–1860 (Cambridge University Press, Cambridge).

Green, William A., 1977, "Caribbean historiography, 1600–1900: The recent tide," Journal of Interdisciplinary History. 7.

Richardson, David, 1975, "Profitability in the Bristol–Liverpool slave trade"; Revue française d'histoire d'outre-mer 62.

Sheridan, R.B., 1965, "The wealth of Jamaica in the eighteenth century": Economic History Review, 2nd series, 43.

Sheridan; R.B., 1968, "The wealth of Jamaica in the eighteenth century:" A rejoinder, Economic History Review, 2nd series, 21.

Smith, Adam, 1937, Wealth of nations (Modern Library, New York).

Sraffa, P., ed., 1951, David Ricardo, works and correspondence (Cambridge University Press, Cambridge).

Thomas, Robert Paul, 1968, "The sugar colonies of the old empire: Profit or loss for Great Britain?'" Economic History Review, 2nd series, 21.

Verlinden, Charles, 1970 The beginnings of modern colonization: Eleven essays with an introduction (Cornell University Press, Ithaca, NY).

Williams, Eric, 1966, Capitalism and slavery (Capricorn Books, New York).

CHAPTER SIX

~

Marx, Slavery, and American Economic Growth*

Feudal societies and market societies with abundant land share a common characteristic: in both, labor has what might be called "direct access" to the means of production. This comes about in the former because principles of commonality govern property relations, in the latter because of the near-free availability of land. Both cases can be viewed as presenting an obstacle to economic development for the same reasons: there is no labor market for a landlord, no source of a surplus, no incentive for investment, no source of return to investors. The solution for feudalism is to "marketize" by extinguishing communal property rights and establishing private ownership. One suggested solution to the abundant land case in a market economy is for government artificially to price land high enough to force workers onto an artificially created labor market. Another "solution" is to establish slavery. Slavery renders workers immobile by naked coercion and allows slave owners to determine the employment of labor by the principles that apply when land is limited.

Marx understood that with free land, equally as in feudalism, economic growth required the separation of labor from access to the means of production: "the secret discovered in the new world by the political economy of the old world, and proclaimed from the house-tops: that the capitalist mode of

---

*This paper deals only with the modern chattel slavery that was introduced into the Atlantic world from the Mediterranean in the late Middle Ages and served as the industrial system of important parts of this world from the sixteenth to the nineteenth centuries.

production and accumulation, and therefore capitalist private property, have for their fundamental condition the annihilation of self-earned property; in other words, the expropriation of the laborer."[1]

This paper is addressed to two audiences. I would like to persuade Marxists that the institution of slavery results in a primitive accumulation of capital and an acceleration of economic growth just as the enclosure movement did and for the same reason. I would like to persuade non-Marxists that because of the abundance of land the New World was economically stagnant before slavery was introduced, that slavery was the foundation of the Atlantic trading system, and provided a very strong impetus to economic growth on both sides of the Atlantic.

Looking at slavery in this context brings out comparisons quite different from other approaches. To the anthropologist, historian, psychologist, or sociologist, fruitful comparisons can be made between modern slave societies and feudal societies; from an economic viewpoint they are antithetical. The anthropologist, historian, psychologist, or sociologist may find feudalism and yeoman agriculture antithetical, but in certain well-defined circumstances, from an economic viewpoint they share fundamental characteristics.

As every school boy knows, before the eighteenth century no European country (and no non-European country) exhibited sustained economic growth in the sense that per capita incomes continued to rise secularly regardless of the rate of population increase. European economies before that grew slowly for long periods only seemingly to hit some sort of ceiling, as in the fourteenth and seventeenth centuries. England was the first economy where per capita incomes kept increasing with rapid population growth, and others followed.

It is a natural question how economies originally develop from a more or less stationary initial state. Modern growth economists are not concerned with this question: they look at population, capital, and technical change as explanatory variables. But they are addressing the world of modern institutions, where private property owners maximize profits in a market system. Some early classical economists (among them Karl Marx) did think about the relation of until institutions to sustained growth; until recently the subject belonged mainly to development economists and economic historians, but today it is a very popular topic.

For Marx it was the transition from feudalism to capitalism that released "social productive powers" by separating labor from access to the means of production. Among the mutual traditional rights and obligations that allocated resources in the feudal age in the absences of private ownership, peasants enjoyed a prescriptive right to the soil in open fields and commons.

Feudal landlords, measuring their wealth in manpower not rent rolls, acquiesced. Marx's story is that the development of a capitalist mentality—spurred in part by rising wool prices at the end of the fifteenth century—encouraged landlords to assert ownership rights, drive the peasants off the commons, and devote the vacated area to profitable sheepwalks. The process of expropriation was accelerated by the disposal of church lands in the Reformation and continued in the Restoration and after the Glorious Revolution until, by the time of Napoleonic enclosure, peasant right of access to arable and commons had disappeared. The violent acts of expropriation of the fifteenth and sixteenth centuries gave way to legislative expropriation with the enclosure acts of the eighteenth and nineteenth centuries.

We are now in a world where land and labor are allocated by markets. Marx writes in his usual tone of moral outrage of the brutal and flagrant robbery of the cultivators' rights; their transformation into beggars, vagabonds, and thieves—"a servile rabble dependent on the pleasure of the landlords"; eventually their virtual enslavement in factories by the vagrancy laws. But what are the consequences for the economy? Marx acknowledges that an agricultural revolution results. The agrarian sector is free to adopt improved methods and division of labor, and exploit economies of scale. Productivity rises: "the soil brought forth as much or more produce than before."

The remodelled agrarian sector produced enough to supply the evicted labor supply that had moved to towns and industry. At the same time, the expulsion of peasants from the land meant the end of rural cottage industry; spinning and weaving moved to factories; the agrarian sector became a market for these industries as the industrial sector became a market for the agrarian output.

The feudal organization of agriculture and the guild regulations of medieval towns had prevented the growth of the economy. Privatization permitted the freed labor to combine with capital, and the result was "the development of the social productive power of labor, division of labor, use of machinery on a large scale." Indeed, according to Marx, "the productive application of the forces of Nature by society" is let loose in the privatization process. We enter into what we might call an era of sustained growth but what Marx called an era of capitalist exploitation and increasing concentration, containing the seeds of its own destruction.

We are now on the familiar ground where the integument bursts asunder, the knell of capitalist private property sounds, and the expropriators are expropriated. All that depends on the rigmarole of Marxian surplus value theory; if that falls we are still left with a Marxian theory of the escape from a bad initial stationary state to a progressive economy.

With the accumulation of empirical historical knowledge and the development of modern economic analysis, this Marxian approach has been restated in contemporary terms, notably by the historian Robert Brenner, the economic historian Jon Cohen, and the economic theorist Martin Weitzman.[2]

Brenner's article, "Agrarian Class Structure and Economic Development in Pre-Industrial Europe," initiated a vigorous debate which "may justifiably lay claim to being one of the most important historical debates of recent years."[3]

Like Marx, Brenner describes a feudal economy where returns to landlords are extracted by extra-economic compulsion, and peasants produce for subsistence on land to which they have prescriptive rights. Like Marx, he argues that this organization sets limits to growth because it precludes specialization, the investment of a surplus, and technological innovation. With population increase, he sees this institutional arrangement leading to declining productivity and ultimately to large-scale crisis. The cure is a reorganization in which the generation and distribution of the landlord surplus is brought into a system of markets, and peasant labor is separated from access to land and is likewise allocated by a market mechanism. The market, so dear to the heart of the neoclassical economist, is also dear to the heart of the Marxist.[4]

Brenner argues that the long-term process of class formation, brought about by redefining property rights, was the principal determinant of the course of European economic history from the late Middle Ages to the nineteenth century, as against the more traditional story which makes demographic change the main causal factor. To Brenner, the pace and pattern of the replacement of feudal property rights determined differing outcomes in England and France, in Eastern and Western Europe. Without denying the significance of demographic change, Brenner sees it as filtered through the dynamics of class formation which then has primary explanatory value. The Brenner debate clearly poses the question of the role of property institutions in economic growth as against the role of changes in population, resources, and technology. Much of the debate, however, has focused on the interpretation of particular historical facts, not about the theoretical model, which is what matters for our purposes here.

Both Marx's and Brenner's formulations present empirical and theoretical problems: empirical problems revolve around interpretation and dating, the theoretical problems revolve around the fuzziness in the specification of exactly what it is about feudalism that capitalism cures. These problems are elucidated in a brilliant paper by Jon Cohen and Martin Weitzman, which has never received the attention it deserves. This neglect may be explained by the methodology and the vocabulary of the Cohen-Weitzman article: the methodology is the model-building of the modern economist, and the vocabulary is mathematics.

Cohen and Weitzman understand that no model can possibly account for all the regional variation, cultural differences, locational advantages, receptiveness to new ideas, and so on, which play a role in historians' descriptions. That is not an argument against model-building, it is an argument for it. Only by stripping away the adventitious can we isolate the essential factors and hope to achieve analytic insight; the use of mathematical specification has resulted in enormous gains in clarity and rigor.

Cohen and Weitzman model the communal world of feudalism and the private property world of capitalism and observe the implications of the transformation from one to the other for national income, economic efficiency, levels of wages and rents, population, and industrialization. That the results of the modeling exercise roughly correspond to historical reality does not prove causality, since so much else is happening. But if a model is based on plausible assumptions, is logically consistent, is compatible with the empirical record, and in a way that is superior to alternative explanations, then we can take its explanatory value seriously.

The picture of the feudal world depicted in the model is familiar from the work of traditional historians: a world of communal ownership and equalized individual rights. A passage from Vinogradoff captures the flavor of the situation:

(Open field agriculture) was a system primarily intended for the purpose of equalizing shares, and it considered every man's rights and property as interwoven with other people's rights and property: it was therefore a system particularly adapted to bring home the superior right of the community as a whole, and the inferior, derivative character of individual rights. Even when the shifting, "ideal" share of the land of the community (i.e., by annual repartition) had given way to the permanent ownership by each member of certain particular scattered strips, this permanent ownership did by no means amount to private property in the Roman or in the modern sense. The communal principle with its equalizing tendency remained still as the efficient force regulating the whole and was strong enough to subject even the lord and the freeholders to its customary influence. By saying this, I do not mean to maintain, of course, that private property was non-existent, that it was not breaking through the communal systems and acting as a dissolvent of it. But the fact remains that the system which prevailed upon the whole during the middle ages appears directly connected in its most important features with ideals of communal ownership and equalized individual rights.[5]

The essence of the enclosure movement was the transformation of a system of communally regulated land to a system of private property. To illustrate the consequence of the transformation, Cohen and Weitzman model first a communal organization and next a private property organization and compare the results.

Consider a single prototype pre-enclosure village occupying a certain quantity of land, For every input of labor there corresponds a maximum output (of various product mixes suitably aggregated). We can draw this relation very simply. The lord's share is set by custom; we deal with it offstage, so to speak; agricultural output is all produced by labor. (*figure 6.1.*) Measure labor on the horizontal axis and total product on the vertical. Total product rises but at a decreasing rate, since each additional laborer has less land to work with. This is jus the common law of diminishing returns. With x' laborers in the village, the total product is R', and each laborer produces R' divided by x', which we can think of as a labor payment; it is measured by the slope OA. If x' were lower, the implicit wage would be higher; and if x' were higher, the implicit wage would be lower.

Now consider the case where the lord establishes ownership rights to the land and becomes a profit-maximizer. He will seek the greatest difference between Total Revenue and Total Cost. The only cost is labor; if the wage is the same as the return to each laborer in the prototype pre-enclosure village in figure 6.1, the total cost curve is a ray from the origin. (figure 6.2.) Maximum profit occurs at a labor input of x* with a revenue of R*; it is measured by the vertical distance between revenue and cost. If you are a historian you can see by eye that Total Revenue minus Total Cost is greatest there; the condition for maximum profits is that the slope of the TR curve (marginal revenue) equal the slope of the TC curve (marginal costs). With fewer laborers, you can add to profits by increasing (and with more laborers, you can add to profit by decreasing) the labor force; at x* you are maximizing profits.

The profit-maximizing landlord produces less output than the communal village, but since he reduces his costs by even more he will gain overall. The difference between Total Revenue and Total Costs achieved by the privatization which destroys the peasants' right to stay on the land and enables the landlord to evict some of them now goes as a surplus to the lord, to do with as he likes. The essence of private property is the right to exclude: the mere movement to privatization depopulates the village and moves the land to a less labor-intensive part of the total product curve. What we observe as depopulation and the replacement of men by sheep are consequences of the change from a communal to a private property world.

This much is simple and even elementary. It is by extending the model from the case where one village is enclosed to the case where all villages are enclosed that Cohen and Weitzman make their fundamental contribution. This further step is too complex to describe here, but the results can be summarized. When village land is enclosed, other things being equal, the general equilibrium model yields the following results:

1. Peasants are displaced from the newly-enclosed land.
2. The standard of living of the working population declines.
3. Rents rise and the surplus increases.
4. Less labor-intensive techniques are used on the newly-enclosed land.
5. The population of other villages rises.
6. New lands are settled.
7. National income is higher.
8. Agricultural output is produced more efficiently.
9. There is a net outflow of labor out of agriculture.
10. Therefore the terms of trade move in favor of agriculture against industry.

Like Brenner, Cohen and Weitzman are not saying that other things like population and technology remained equal: the model's results just establish that if the only change in the economy were a move from communal to private property, these changes would result. That the model captures a significant part of the explanation of economic growth between feudalism and capitalism is shown by what I believe to be a closer fit to the empirical record than that of alternative explanations.[6] In Marxian terms the original seizure of peasants' rights by the new profit-maximizing landlord generated a stream of profits for the first time (hence "primitive accumulation"), which could be saved and accumulated as capital, beginning the process of sustained growth, at least for a while.

What is there about the newly-discovered lands of the western hemisphere that bears the slightest resemblance to feudalism? Although (at least in New England) initially land was managed in common, this economic organization did not persist, and the evidence of private property and a functioning market system from early on is very strong.[7] Nevertheless, in the emptied lands of the western hemisphere each man had access to land just as each feudal peasant did: the peasant because of ascriptive right to a customarily fixed amount of land, the free farmer because of the abundance of land. The consequences of free land have been spun out by many writers: for example, a Dutch ethnographer, a Russian historian, English classical economists, and here again have been translated into the language of modern economics by Evsey Domar.[8]

In a simple agricultural society where land and labor are all that are required for production because capital is either unneeded or too rudimentary to be costly (the assumptions Marx makes), then if land is freely abundant each man will acquire a piece for himself and go to work for himself. Why would he share the proceeds of his labor by paying rent to a landlord if he could keep them to himself? If the landlord were to try to lure him into service by paying more, there would be nothing left for the landlord. So if land is so available, no man will be found working for another unless by coercion. Notice that this simple sentence encapsulates the history of the United States: land was available; in the North men were not usually working for others; in the South men were found working for others and it was by coercion. Free land will be characterized either by family farms or by landed aristocracies with slaves. Without slavery, feudalism and free land grant direct access to the means of production to the peasant and farmer, respectively.

Domar's exposition states the free land case in the simple terms we used above. Figure 6.2 illustrated the case of the profit-maximizing landlord when land is limited. As in that case, the landlord receives the value of the average product times the number of laborers, and his costs are the (lower) value of the marginal product times the number of laborers. The difference is the landlord's rent, and it comes about because of the curved shape of the total product curve. Total product increases at a decreasing rate where land is limited, because each additional laborer has less land to work with; thus the product of the last laborer is smaller than the average. Where land is without limit, the total curved product curve does not have this curved shape. Let the x-axis again measure a bundle of labor, and the y-axis again measure total product. With unlimited land this "curve" is a straight line from the origin. Every laborer can now work as many acres as he gives the best contribution of output and effort. Then, as more workers are added, this package is reproduced so that the total product is just proportional to total labor. The last laborer is paid the marginal product, but the marginal product in this case equals the average product. Once laborers are paid their marginal product no surplus remains for the landlord, and the usual disadvantages obtain.

To summarize the argument to this point: there is no land market and no labor market in pure feudalism or the pure free land case. If land is commonly available in a market economy labor is unconstrained, the returns to free labor exhaust the total product, just as the returns to peasant labor exhaust the total product of the village. If the free laborer or the peasant can be refused access to the land, then land becomes a valuable commodity, a surplus will accrue to the landowner, a labor supply will be available to match it, and we move to a surplus-generating economy. The enclosure movement denied peasants direct access to land, and the new agrarian society remodeled on private property lines led to economic development. This is Marx's story.

Where land is free, the laborer can be deprived of free access to land if the sovereign power arbitrarily prices land beyond his means. This was the colonization scheme Edward Gibbon Wakefield proposed for Australia and New Zealand. But an alternative "final solution" to the free land case was at hand. Slavery denies labor access to land by direct coercion, labor becomes a commodity owned by the planter class, establishing conditions for a surplus, a supply of investible funds matched by a labor supply, providing an incentive for foreign as well as domestic investment, and a source of return on that investment. Economic growth in the colonial period in the western hemisphere was concentrated at times and places where slavery was introduced. European economic success, proceeding for its own reasons, was also accelerated by success in the New World. Slavery, equally with the enclosure movement, was a source of primitive capital accumulation in Marx's words, and a vital impetus to economic growth in the words of non-Marxists.

The Founding Fathers understood from the first that the consequence of free land and free labor in America would be the replication of small family farms across the landscape. Jefferson favored that outcome, and Hamilton deplored it.

Hamilton's economic ideas were influenced by Hume, and perhaps Hume accustomed him to the belief that economic development would require government intervention.[9] Certainly Hamilton had the concept of primitive accumulation. Hume argued that agricultural economies lack incentives for labor to work beyond subsistence because there are no "luxuries" (industrial goods) to buy. The economy as a whole consumes its income, leaving nothing available for investment, industrialization, or military power. Were there such goods, the supply of labor would increase, national product would rise, the nation could industrialize, and guns could be had without giving up butter. Hume's strategy to achieve this end involved increasing the money supply; the price level would rise with a lag, meanwhile real product would increase.

Hamilton shared Hume's view that agricultural economies are stagnant. He feared that there was no source of capital for the new nation, and an interventionist state would have to adopt a tariff policy and a national debt to solve the problem. By encouraging domestic industry, tariffs will lead to development through import-substitution. A national debt will provide a source of capital directly, he thought. Did Hamilton not realize that domestically-held debt would merely replace—"crowd out"—private invest-ment? He did visualize that foreigners, who would not otherwise invest in the private sector of the new country, would buy the government-backed bonds. Hamilton's version of primitive accumulation explicitly involved foreign capital imports.

Jefferson and Madison had different aims for American society. Jefferson understood that free land would lead to a nation of family farmers, and that was what Jefferson wanted: not because he was anti-urban, anti-merchant, or anti-speculator (although he was all of those things), but because of his ideal of an egalitarian society and his devotion to liberty. The disappearance of yeoman agriculture would result in Marx's "servile rabble dependent on the pleasure of employers," at a cost to political liberty. Jefferson wanted no part of economic progress if it increased inequality and led to the unmerited enrichment of speculators. Like borrowers everywhere, he firmly opposed the class to whom he owed money. The mere idea of debt was distasteful to him. (It is remarkable that Jefferson never realized that the only thing worse than debt is not having anybody to borrow from.)

The Jeffersonian ideal was the economic organization of the northern states. But there were no Monticellos in Vermont or New Hampshire. Did it never occur to him that the cultivated, cultured, leisured life he enjoyed was founded on slave labor?

Neither Jefferson's hopes nor Hamilton's fears were realized in the late eighteenth and early nineteenth century: the introduction of slavery had moved the western hemisphere colonies in a different direction. Aside from the mining industries of Peru and Mexico, before the introduction of African slavery western hemisphere colonists everywhere were waging a losing battle for survival. In the West Indies, settlers growing tobacco, indigo, cotton, co-coa, or ginger on small plots with a few servants and slaves, failed to establish viable colonies. In New England farmers struggled to make a living from the stony soil. The Middle States were a kinder environment, and in the Upper South a promising tobacco culture was in its infancy.

. Within a decade after the introduction of sugar into Barbados, the small holders were replaced by large plantations and the free white labor force was replaced by black slaves. One West Indian island after another underwent the same transformation over the course of the eighteenth century.

Expansion of Chesapeake tobacco depended on slave labor, as did the cul-tivation of rice, indigo, and cotton of the Lower South. And New Englanders found in the Caribbean a market for their grain, livestock, and their shipping industry. The New England merchant class has its origin in its connection to the slave society of the Caribbean, and the wealth and growth of British America is causally connected with slavery.

All this is not to argue that slavery was a necessary condition for success: those yeoman farmers would and did in time develop a growing economy (with, it must be admitted, the aid of Hamilton's idea of a tariff). But the actual historical origin of American growth in the early period lay with slavery, and the Atlantic trading system of the eighteenth century was directly based upon it. Indeed not much moved in the Atlantic except slaves, the products of slaves, capital and supplies to slave societies, and goods and services bought with the proceeds. Capital was invested from Europe, most of it to the slave regions. And this Atlantic trade is not unconnected with the British story.

English economic growth occurred in a context where land and labor were increasingly allocated by market mechanisms. When population increased in the eighteenth century, instead of running into diminishing returns England responded with technical change in agriculture (especially by folding livestock into the arable rotation). Such adaptation would have been impossible without the remodelling of property rights. What declined was not the absolute amount of labor on the land but the share of agrarian labor in the burgeoning population. With approximately the same amount of agrarian labor, productivity increased so much that almost until the middle of the nineteenth century the vastly increased population could be fed without recourse to large-scale imports except in unusual years. The augmented labor supply was able to produce industrial goods, at first of a rudimentary kind by rudimentary methods. But it was into this setting that the technological innovations of the late eighteenth and early nineteenth centuries took place.

The eighteenth century brought England an Industrial Revolution as it brought France the French Revolution. In France the peasant had retained a grip on his holdings, and the land-owning class lived to a great extent off the traditionally set charges on the peasantry, not by themselves combining productive factors in the service of profit-maximization. Not adjustment but conflict resulted.

The Atlantic trading system based on slavery had a role in the English case too. Over the eighteenth century the mean annual growth rate of British exports increased markedly, and most of the incremental commodity exports were going to North America and the West Indies. The most dynamic and innovative British industries were those dependent on American demand.[10]

As show in the two figures below, Marx's primitive accumulation story helps explain the escape from stagnation in Britain; the institution of slavery,

Total Product   A

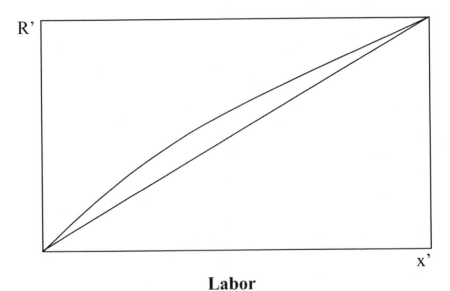

Figure 6.1.

Total Product   A

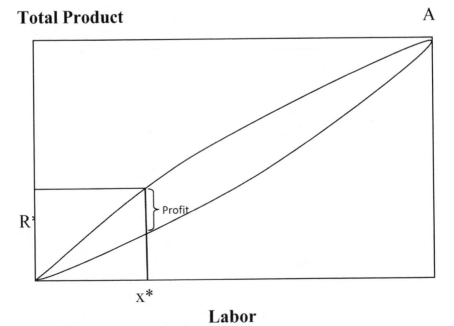

Figure 6.2.

equally a source of primitive accumulation, underlies American escape from stagnation and contributes to British eighteenth century growth as well.

Notes

1. Karl Marx, *Capital: A Critique of Political Economy*, Volume I, trans, from the third German edition by Samuel Moore and Edward Aveling and edited by Frederick Engels, revised by Ernest Unterman (Chicago, 1906). All references in this paper are to Part VIII, "The So-called Primitive Accumulation," comprising chapters xxxvi–xxxiii.

2. Robert Brenner, "Agrarian Class Structure and Economic Development in Pre-industrial Europe," *Past and Present*, 70 (February 1976). Jon S. Cohen and Martin L. Weitzman, "A Marxian Model of Enclosures," *Journal of Development Economics*, 1 (1975). See also M. Dobb, *Studies in the Development of Capitalism* (London, 1946).

3. T.H. Aston and C.H.E. Philpin, eds., *The Brenner Debate: Agrarian Class Structure and Economic Development in Pre-industrial Europe* (Cambridge, England, 1985), vii. Brenner asserts that "attempts at economic model-building are necessarily doomed from the start precisely because, most crudely stated, it is the structure of class relations, of class power, which will determine the manner and degree to which particular demographic and commercial changes will affect long-term trends in the distribution of income and economic growth—and not vice versa." In fact, Cohen and Weitzman used economic model-building precisely to analyze the class structure that concerns Brenner.

4. See particularly D. C. North and R. P. Thomas, *The Rise of the Western World* (Cambridge, 1973).

5. Quoted in Cohen and Weitzman, op. cit., p. 297. This quotation brings out clearly the value of abstracting from qualifications, exceptions, and "noise" to isolate the essence of medieval property relations. Modelling pure the pure communal case and the pure free land case enables us to isolate the effects of changes in property relations. But no one believes, as Vinogradoff makes clear that the pure cases prevailed literally.

6. Persuasive arguments against the demographic explanation are found in Cohen and Weitzman, op. cit., 328–30.

7. For a good review of the literature, see Gordon S. Wood, "Inventing American Capitalism," *New York Review of Books*, June 9, 1994.

8. Edward Gibbon Wakefield, *Collected Works*, ed. M.F. Lloyd Prichard (Auckland, 1969). Evsey D. Domar, "The Causes of Slavery and Serfdom: A Hypothesis," *Journal of Economic History*, XXX. For references to Nieboer and Kluchevsky, see Domar.

9. See Stanley Elkins and Eric McKitrick, *The Age of Federalism: The Early Republic, 1788-1800* (New York and Oxford, 1993) for an excellent discussion of Hamilton and Jefferson and a summary and evaluation of the literature.

10. See P.K. O'Brien and S.L. Engerman, "Exports and the Growth of the British Economy from the Glorious Revolution to the Peace of Amiens," in B.L. Solow, ed., *Slavery and the Rise of the Atlantic System* (Cambridge, England, 1991). *The Transition to Plantation Slavery: The Case of the British West Indies.*

CHAPTER SEVEN

The Transition to Plantation Slavery: The Case of the British West Indies

In 1623, an English merchant named Jobson told a Mandingo slave trader that "we were a people who did not deal in such commodities, neither did we buy or sell one another, or any that had our own shapes." Fifty years later the Royal African Company was chartered, and before the slave trade was abolished in 1807, England had transported two million slaves to her colonies in the Western Hemisphere. The revival of an institution which had virtually disappeared from Western Europe in the tenth century requires explanation. Why did slavery reappear at a particular time and in particular places? Does a series of historical accidents explain its reemergence or was it determined by systematic, analyzable elements? This paper discusses the transition to slavery in the British West Indies as a contribution toward answering the wider questions.

Thinking about modern slavery as an industrial system and not as an abstract philosophical problem has been the province of the economist. Modern economic historians view slaves as a factor of production and locate the economics of slavery in the textbook chapters on distribution and production and marginal products. The essential economic difference between free and slave labor is that the former is rented for a price (called a wage), while the latter is purchased out-right by the firm who then enjoys his services.

The rate of return on a slave depends upon the purchase price and the value of the net product (gross product minus maintenance). Maintenance, Hicks reminds us, should not be viewed as a fixed sum. "There is always a

111

choice between investing capital in the maintenance of the future productivity of existing assets, and investing it and buying new ones; or putting it
aside to buy new ones at an earlier date than would have been necessary if
the other course had been followed."[1] A positive slave price measures the difference between the present value of the future stream of services the slave is
expected to provide and the present value of the maintenance costs. So long
as the former exceeds the latter, slavery is profitable to the owner.

The firm chooses between hiring free labor and buying slaves in precisely
the same way it chooses between hiring labor and buying a machine. The
cost per period of the free labor is the wage. The cost per period of the slave
is maintenance plus interest and depreciation. If slave prices or interest rates
are high, the cost of the slave can greatly exceed maintenance. If the price
of the slave should equal maintenance, nothing will remain toward capital
costs, and the supply of slaves will dry up. Thus, the cost of slaves depends
on maintenance and capital costs, and the price of free labor depends on
supply and demand.

From this viewpoint, slaves and free labor are alternatives whose costs depend on the market, and neither one nor the other will be cheaper a *priori*. In
a competitive world, slave and free labor will be hired until the price of each
is brought into equivalence with its marginal revenue product (where the
slave's is net of maintenance and capital costs). Under some circumstances
slaves will be more expensive than free labor and under others the contrary.
Using slave labor need not violate efficiency conditions, and there is no
reason to expect slave economies to wither and die.

The classical economists looked at slavery in quite a different way. To
Adam Smith a slave is never to be preferred to free labor on economic
grounds: slaves produce less and cost more to maintain. How can they possibly cost more since they need only be kept at subsistence? In his enthusiasm
for free labor, Smith argues that the funds for slave maintenance will be
administered by a negligent minter or careless overseer. Such people seem
to him inherently inefficient: "disorders generally prayed in the economy of
the rich." Costing more, slaves produce less because the have no incentive
to work.

This experience of all ages and nations, I believe, demonstrates that the
work done by slaves, though it appears to cost only their maintenance is
in the end the dearest of any. A person, who can acquire no property, can
have no other interest but to eat as much and to labor as little as possible.
Whatever work he does beyond what is sufficient to purchase his own maintenance, can be squeezed out of him by violence only, and not by any interest
of his own.[2]

While the modern statement says that the choice between slave and free depends on the respective differences between discounted future income and discounted future costs, Smith says free labor will always show the greater difference: income will be greater on incentive grounds and costs lower on "wasteful overseer" grounds. If one disregards the "wasteful overseer" story as inherently implausible, costs of both kinds of labor to a classical economist will be equal because the Malthusian population story drives free labor to subsistence. In this case it is only the productivity differentials that sustain the view that free labor is cheaper.

Adam Smith's authority enshrined his view in the minds of generations of Britons. It was dear to the hearts of many Abolitionists and played a role in their manifestoes. "That slave labor is dearer than free has almost passed into an axion,"[3] Merivale told his Oxford students, as he proceeded to lecture on the profitability of free labor. No more than Adam Smith could he conceive that more productivity might be "squeezed out by violence" than by the prospect of acquiring property. His explanation comes from the cost side.

Free labor is reduced to subsistence wages in the classical scheme because the variable factor (labor) is added to the fixed factor (land) until diminishing returns drives down the per capita product to subsistence. Old settled countries are already at this Malthusian equilibrium, but so long as free land is available—and a unit of land can be added with every new unit of labor there is no tendency to diminishing returns and subsistence wages. Here the slave's labor will be cheaper since he costs only subsistence, and free labor's wage exceeds it. However, once the free population becomes so dense that its wages are also driven to subsistence slavery will come to an end. Its profitability depends on free soil, declines as population rises, and reaches a limit when all the soil is occupied. "Towards this limit every community is approximating, however slowly."

Merivale's statement has predictive power: slavery occurs only where there is free soil and disappears when population fills up the vacant land. Few modern historians have employed this theory to explain the origin of modern slavery, although I have argued elsewhere for some connection. So far as I know, no modern writer argues for a limit to slavery, and there is no economic theory of decline in the sense of Merivale's. However, many have followed Merivale in stressing the land/labor ratio in determining post-slavery economic adjustment.

The neoclassical statement offers not a theory with predictive power but a set of empty boxes, which must be filled with numbers to determine the appearance or disappearance of slavery. For the most part, the boxes that modern economic historians have chosen to fill contain the prices of slave and free labor: the introduction of slavery is ascribed to the relative cheapness of slave labor compared with indentured servants. "Considerable evidence indicates that the labor forces of the British colonies that became agricultural staple producers and exporters went through a series of unidentifiable periods as a result of systematic changes in the relative cost of servant and slave labor."[4]

This "supply-side" approach to slavery can be illustrated by a few examples. Robert P. Thomas and Richard N. Bean, explicitly rejecting productivity differentials, argue that indentured labor cost the same in the Chesapeake and the Caribbean, but that in the Caribbean slaves were 15–20 percent cheaper, owing to transport costs.[5] In the initial situation, indentured servants were the low-cost labor. Then in 1640–45, rising English wages increased the cost of indentured servants, while slave prices were either steady or falling. This caused the British West Indies to adopt slavery, but in the Chesapeake the price of indentures, though rising, remained below that of slaves. Not until slave prices began to fall in the 1680s, did the Chesapeake begin its transition. When slave prices subsequently rose in the 1690s, they were matched by indentured labor prices, so no reversal occurred.

A more sophisticated approach, due to Gemery and Hogendorn, assumes that free or indentured labor is more productive than slave but that this advantage is overborne by the cheapness of slave labor and the possible capital gains associated with it.[6] In the initial situation both kinds of labor are used. Then, according to these authors, total demand for labor increased with the rise of labor-intensive agriculture associated with staple crops. The supply of white labor was inelastic and that of black labor very elastic, thus explaining the shift. Supply elasticity calls the tune, and the shift to staple production is exogenous.

Another supply-side story is told by Russell Menard.[7] He argues that a leftward shift in the supply curve of indentures accounted for the shift to slaves in the Chesapeake, and not a fall in slave prices associated with the break-up of the Royal African Company monopoly, as had been traditionally alleged. Slavery in the Chesapeake antedated a dependable supply of cheap slaves by a generation, according to Menard.

If relative prices are the key variable, then the economic historian will concentrate on English wages, the decline in English population growth rates in the late seventeenth century, changes in transport costs, monopoly pricing in slave trade, mortality rates of slaves, and similar factors as fundamental elements. This has indeed been the case in much of the American literature.

The traditional historians of the West Indies have instead identified the key variable as the choice of crop.[8] To them slavery goes with sugar. They depict the first generation of colonists as small holders growing tobacco, cotton, indigo, and ginger with white indentured labor and some black slaves. When sugar was introduced the islands were one by one transformed into large plantations with almost wholly black labor forces. For the most part these authors make no effort to view the change as the outcome of an economic process. Unique discrete historical events provide *ad hoc* explanations. The Bridenbaughs and Sheridan both provide immensely satisfying portrayals of the transition, rich in detail and panoramic in scope, but neither attempts a systematic analysis.

Dunn's account of Barbados is an excellent example of the ad hoc explanation. "The Dutch in Brazil taught the English in Barbados how to make sugar. The timing was perfect for no other Caribbean island as yet produced sugar for the European market, and Brazil was a battleground between the Dutch and the Portuguese. . . . The Dutch obligingly showed the English how to process the cane, supplied them with African slaves on easy terms, and sold their product in Amsterdam" (p. 61). The Dutch appear in this as in other versions as a *dues ex machina*, obligingly assisting and even "subsidizing" (p. 65) the Barbadians. The fortuitous introduction of sugar led to monoculture. Economies of scale increased the optimal size of plantation and either eliminated small proprietors or drove them into small plots of marginal land. There are plenty of white indentured servants about, Dunn observes, "but the striking thing is how eagerly the planters plunged into the slaveholding business" (pp. 67–68). Why? The English, lacking the long Iberian experience with Moslem and African slavery, originally found it an alien institution. But white indentured servants proved troublesome, masters brutal, servants rebellious. "As this point, the example of Brazilian slavery was decisive." (p. 72). Suddenly servants proved fractious and providentially another labor farce turned up?

Dunn's account of the change to slavery on Barbados contains many coincidences; it is not a wholly convincing account; it by no means fully convinces so excellent a historian as Professor Dunn, who finds that puzzling elements remain.

Neither the free land nor the relative price story nor the *ad hoc* explanation is sufficient in explaining the transition to plantation slavery in the British West Indies. A snapshot of the islands in 1650, would find Barbados launched into plantation slavery, St. Christopher covered by a dense population of poor whites, the island "worn out by reason of the multitudes that were on it," Antigua barely settled and fearing depopulation; most householders on Nevis in subsistence farming; and Jamaica in Spanish hands. A generation later Barbados was dominated by 175 large plantations owners;

among the four Leeward Islands there were fewer than two dozen planters with more than sixty slaves: the Jamaican economy was the home of marauding and plundering buccaneers, and it would take Jamaica 60 years from the expulsion of the Spanish to reach the Barbadian sugar output of 1655.

Every author has his own Golden Age for the West Indies. Sheridan's Golden Age is in the 1660s; Dunn's book on the rise of the planter class ends in 1713; Pares's Golden Age is in the 1640s; Parry and Sherlock's between the War of Jerkin's Ear and the Seven Years' War—when the Golden Age of the French West Indies commences. This is not because these authors are mistaken, but because islands developed at different times. This causes problems for the kind of explanations we have considered above.

If "systematic changes in the relative cost of servant and slave labor" drive the transition, all the islands would be expected to shift at the same time (as Bean and Thomas recognize). Only transport costs would account for different prices facing each island, and between nearby islands they will be small. It would thus require a contorted and complex choreography of price changes to account for transitions at widely different dates. If the shift to slave labor occurs not merely at different times but is associated with certain crops ("staples" in Gemery and Hogendorn) or with different sizes of holding (as Fogel and Engerman's view of scale economies in slavery implies), then more is going on than changes in the servant/slave price ratio.

It is misleading to think of the British West Indies planter as simply choosing between two alternative streams of labor: one of indentured servants, driven by demographic and wage conditions in England: the other of slaves, driven by the costs and organization of the trade in Africa. White labor in the Caribbean, in addition to indentured servants, was supplied by convicts, vagabonds, deserters, and deportees. Barbados is also a verb, meaning "to deport". Royalists, Irish, veterans of Monmouth's Rebellion, occasional Quakers and even some Scottish Covenanters were shipped there, as well as kidnap victims. Moreover, a population of white servants was already in the colonies before the transition to slavery: some islands were densely populated in the pre-sugar era. In the same way, Africa was not the exclusive source of slaves since some of the early imports into one island came from another island. The earliest slave imports into North America included slaves from the West Indies too.

Indeed it seems to me implausible that English society adopted slavery as an industrial system, with its revolutionary remodeling of social institutions and social psychology, because of small relative price changes in the same way that society shifts from oil to gas and back.

In the following section I propose a tentative explanation of the adoption of slavery in the British West Indies. I should like to stress the preliminary nature of the results, but I think it is clear what direction future research will take. The elements of my explanation will differ from those discussed above. In contrast to the relative price side, I emphasize productivity differentials. Once they are admitted the cost side no longer is decisive.

The main point is that the relative productivity of slave and free labor varies by crop and can vary widely. This can be illustrated by an example. When Gray and Wood calculated the cost of running a fifty acre mixed farm producing corn, beans, sweet potatoes, livestock, and wood in colonial Georgia, they found under reasonable assumptions that the rate of return with slaves exceeded the prevailing rate in the economy by modest amounts and that with servants fell short.[9] But when they attempted to assemble estimates for a one hundred acre rice plantation, they were unable to do so: not a single rice plantation had a nonslave labor force. Thus the profitability of slave and free labor on the small mixed farm is a consequence of moderate differences in productivity, food costs, and supervisory wages. It is hard to believe that society would remodel its institutions to capture the gains that would ensue from a shift to slavery on such farms. If rice production, on the other hand, was an extremely profitable enterprise that could only be carried on in the Western hemisphere with a slave labor force, the motivation for drastic social change becomes more plausible. What Gray and Wood found for rice is true for sugar: production of (cane) sugar by free labor has been extremely rare in recorded history until relatively modern times.

Two reasons are usually advanced for the advantages for slaves in crops like rice, sugar, and cotton. In large units slaves are more productive because of their ability to work effectively in gangs. Some associate this with cultural and technical conditions in Africa. I think some semantic pussyfooting may be going on here: one misses the forthright admission that slavery is a coerced state and the costs of enforcing it can be considerable. Adam Smith, Merivale, and the rest considered them prohibitive. But for crops using gang labor and for crops difficult to sabotage, costs of coercion will be low: one overseer with a whip can "supervise" a gang of one hundred slaves as it moves across a one hundred-acre field, holing, planting, fertilizing, or harvesting canes. Imagine the costs of coercion on a fifty-acre mixed farm, with one or two slaves performing a variety of tasks, requiring skill and versatility, in a variety of places. (Still some room may remain for cultural characteristics—Amerindians were clearly not productive in the same circumstances.)

Another advantage of slaves in crops like sugar results from the aversion of free labor toward the rigorous discipline involved in their production. Pares has called sugar production "a factory in a field". It required labor discipline appropriate to production-line techniques in a world in which such methods were unknown even in industry. Free labor would thus require a premium wage before it would engage in such work. Since slaves do not have the option of demanding such premia they will be cheaper also on the grounds. The premium can either be subtracted from the value productivity of the free or added to the cost side: in either case slave labor is more advantageous for this reason.

We may visualize then a range of crops, each with different productivity differentials between slave and free labor. In some crops, like sugar, slave productivity will greatly exceed that of free labor; in others, like cotton, slave advantage may perhaps be more moderate; in still others the productivity of free labor may be the greater. This last is the case for Smith, Merivale, Bean and Thomas, and Gemery and Hogendorn. Where the slave can express his reluctance for forced labor, where foot-dragging and sabotage are had to detect, costs of coercion will be high. It is perhaps unlikely at any plausible differentials in the relative prices of free and slave labor that the Swiss would have adopted slavery for the clock-making industry—it would take one to watch one (no pun intended). It is no accident that prisoners are used in chain gangs for unskilled labor, like stone breaking and road construction. Indeed if relative prices moved in exactly the same way in New Hampshire and South Carolina, it is not hard to see on these grounds why one would shift to slavery as an industrial system and the other would not. If slaves are extremely cheap of course they may be used where their productivity is greatly inferior—one thinks of certain slave occupations in Brazil—but otherwise we can expect slavery to be concentrated in crops where it has large productivity advantages.

Thus the demand for slaves is in part derived from the demand for particular commodities, and shifts in world demand for them and the elasticity of that demand will be an explanatory factor for the adoption of slavery. Sugar is the commodity that drives the Caribbean transition. It is not just that demand for labor increases and slave labor is more elastically supplied than free when staple production begins—as Galenson and Gemery and Hogendorn have it—but that slave and free labor cease to be good substitutes once sugar production is begun. An elastic supply of slave labor is a necessary condition but not a sufficient one, and it cannot explain the adoption of slavery.

At any given level of world demand, sugar will be supplied from various sources according to their cost levels. Since we identify sugar as the slave crop par excellence in the Caribbean, we will find some clues in its production characteristics. It is useful to think of alternative sugar sources as mines:

each begins with a certain cost of extraction owing to natural characteristics of soil and climate, but as production continues over time, cost curves drift upward as the nutrients of virgin soil are exhausted.[10] After all, this is what is meant by soil exhaustion: when Barbadian planters in the 1680s, complained that their soil was worn out, they meant only that it required more inputs of labor and fertilizer to maintain previous output levels. Thus, at stable demand, low-cost producers supply sugar and require slaves; if demand rises, higher-cost producers can come onto the market. A given location can become a profitable sugar producer and demander of slaves merely because another location's cost curves have risen. It can be an important supplier in its low-cost era, and lose market share as its costs rise over time, and can revive again either because demand increases or other suppliers lose their advantage or disappear from the market altogether.

In my view, the Caribbean historians are right to associate slavery with sugar, and the association is explicable in terms of simple economic elements. It is not possible to say what the history of modern slavery would have been without sugar, but it is perfectly possible to wonder. A third of the Africans shipped to the New World went to Brazil, a colony founded on sugar; a third to the English and French sugar islands; some significant part of the remainder went to Cuba in its sugar era.

A non-specialist may wonder whether the Chesapeake experience can truly be called a transition to slavery. Quantitatively the ratio of blacks to whites never reached above 50 percent except in a few counties. Qualitatively "servants and slaves worked together in the early years of plantation society, drank together, often lived together, sharing the same life, the same hardships, the same abuse . . . The picture which emerges . . . is one of a rather genial mingling of white servants, black slaves, and free persons."[11] Later on, in the second half of the eighteenth century, slave shares increased and racial lines were sharply drawn, but this is long after the transition period identified by the writers cited earlier. Moreover, as Clemens has shown, tobacco growing gave way to grain farming on Maryland's Eastern Shore over the course of the eighteenth century, and slaves began to leave the region.[12] For the origin of slavery as an enduring industrial system in the United States, South Carolina and Georgia are perhaps more promising candidates, and rice and cotton more promising sources than tobacco.[13]

Barbados's shift to a slave economy is the best documented of all the British sugar islands. She succeeded Brazil as the world's premier producer in the decade of the 1650s. The Census of 1680 shows a fully developed sugar/slave plantation economy on Barbados, and travelers' accounts from the 1650s describe the complete clearing of the island, its gardenlike appearance, and its devotion to sugar. But already in 1668, Lord Willoughby, the Royal Governor, had written the Council of Trade in London that the island "renders not by two-thirds its former production by the acre." Twenty years later the Barbadians were exporting along with sugar their complaints about decreasing profits.[14]

Brazil had held predominance in world sugar production for a century before Barbados appeared on the scene. Her production increased steadily from 1550 to 1650, when a decline set in lasting for half a century. (A recovery in 1700–50 was then followed by years of steady decline which only was reversed in the nineteenth century.) In Brazil's heyday sugar was a luxury commodity for the tables of the rich, and consequently demand was quite inelastic. As late as 1783, Lord Sheffield was saying that "the consumption of sugar may increase considerably. It is scarcely known in half Europe. . . ." England was the first place and the eighteenth century the first time of widespread sugar consumption. The English consumed in 1800, nearly fifteen times more than in 1700, far surpassing any other country on a per capita basis.[15]

Edel has argued persuasively that the shift from Brazil to the West Indies did not occur because the island hitherto lacked colonists, or slaves, or the potential knowledge of sugar, or the know-how of the Dutch.[16] All these elements of a sugar industry, especially the presence of the Dutch, had been present in the Caribbean well before the 1650s. The real question would be: why did the Dutch (and others) invest in sugar in another place at a particular time?

This is my tentative answer. The British islands that were occupied from the 1620s were principally producing tobacco. In the 1630s, tobacco prices collapsed from overproduction, leaving the colonists in crisis.[17] They shifted to a variety of crops, of which sugar was only one and indigo another. Sugar prices began rising in the 1640s, tobacco prices remained low, and indigo prices declined precipitously. It seems reasonable to expect colonists' minds to turn toward sugar, and it is in this decade that sugar is pioneered in Barbados. Prices continued high until the late 1650s.

The fragmentary data we have on prices, production, and costs suggest that Barbadian sugar production responded quickly to profit opportunities, but that the increased demand was too inelastic for the combined production of both Brazil and Barbados to be maintained. Brazilian costs were higher, her producers lost their northern European markets to Barbados, and Brazilian sugar production entered a period of decline. Thus, the increased demand for sugar was met by a large supply from Barbados and a shift of some former Brazilian production to that island. The selection of Barbados over St. Christopher for sugar expansion is probably explained by the unsettled conditions on that island, which the English shared with the French and Caribs. Perhaps it is not too far-fetched to suggest that the state of demand also limited the investment in sugar: had more production held out the promise of large profits, might not the English have attempted a military settlement on St. Christopher? They tried just that in 1655, when Cromwell sent the expedition to conquer Santo Domingo for the commercial gains envisioned.

The success of Barbados coincided with a change of commercial policy in the British West Indies. The English knew the islands fifty years before colonization. The Elizabethan policy had featured plundering and privateering. Colonization began in 1623, on St. Christopher, but St. Christopher was not a colony of the English state but belonged to Sir Thomas Warner. Crown policy was to make grants of proprietorships and to leave administrative and economic activity unregulated by state power. One consequence of economic laissez-faire of course was that the Caribbean became in the first half of the seventeenth century "a Dutch Lake." After realizing the great economic potential of the area the English government resolved to exploit it by bringing the colonies under direct governmental control and by limiting commercial access to English nationals. Not only were existing colonies to be exploited this way but English possessions were to be augmented by the capture of Spanish. Such was the Western Design. The acts embodying the new commercial code in 1650 were the forerunners of the Navigation Acts which ruled British foreign economic policy until the nineteenth century. However the mere determination, to develop other islands as profitably as Barbados was not enough to ensure that outcome. The full fruition of the new policy would not occur for another century.

"If seventeenth-century Barbados shows us a sugar colony in its prime, the Leeward Islands were sugar colonies still in their infancy."[18] Overpopulated and impoverished by the tobacco crises, St. Christopher was described by a visitor of 1645, as "the rains of a flourishing place." Antigua and Montserrat were barely secure settlements. Only Nevis was producing much sugar, and most of her population still lived on small tobacco farms.

During their development the four Leeward Islands—St. Christopher, Nevis, Montserrat, and Antigua—suffered wars with the French in 1666–67, 1689–97, 1702–13. They were occupied and sacked; the Irish settlers and Indians were rebellious; they were visited by drought and hurricanes. Yet the chronicle of these disasters provides no chronology for their development pattern. For this it is necessary to look directly at economic data.

After the Peace of Breda in 1667, the Leeward Islands succeeded in getting their own civil government, and reports of Governors and Census compilations let us glimpse their economy. Not until the second decade of the eighteenth century could the Leeward Islands be called a developed slave plantation society.

In 1672, Governor Wheler, returning to England, reported that tiny Nevis was the "whole strength" of the Leeward Islands; Montserrat was occupied by Irish "of no great courage and discipline" in Antigua the men "are generally very mean and live much scattered."[19] Only Nevis had any school or church. The prospects for sugar profits were bad. Christopher Jeaffreson who came to St. Christopher to found a sugar plantation in 1676 was ruined by 1685.[20] Writing to a Mend, he repents his investment:

"Let us consider the extreame low rates sugar now beares, with the small likelyhood of its rising and whether indigo, whose price dayly rises is not like to be a better commodity. It is produced with less charge, made with less trouble, and with less danger of hurricane. Bearing two or three crops per annum, and sometimes four or five cuttings, it is my opinion it would turn to a very good account, better than sugar. Were I upon the plantation knowing what I now know, I would plant indigo, the profits of which the planters understand but halfe. . . ."

The demand that sustained the sugar boom in Barbados did not hold out good prospects for expansion. And the economy of Antigua did not yet turn in that direction. Its economic structure in 1678 can be seen in table 7.1 from the following calculations made from Governor Stapletons's census of that year:

Table 7.1.

Number of holdings	Slaves per holding
288	0
133	1-5
19	5-10
13	10 and up

Over half of the Antiguans held no slaves at all, most slave holders had fewer than five, the Governor had the most (forty). White population exceeded black (10,408 to 8,849) on the four Leeward Islands; only on Nevis did blacks exceed whites and then only by 3,849 to 3,521. The small farmers with a slave or two and a servant or two were not producing much sugar in 1678.

In the 1680s the Royal African Company sent almost no slaves to Nevis to reduce outstanding debt, and the islanders continually sent home petitions for lower taxes, describing their poor situation. They were still trying to attract indentured servants.

The next Census returns for 1707 and 1708 show a different picture. Blacks now outnumber whites overall in the Leeward Islands (23,500 to 7,311), and on every individual island, but more that half the blacks live in Antigua. Antigua had 12,960 slaves in 1708 the other islands thus average around 3,500 each. If we consider "able men" as an admittedly defective proxy of holdings, Antigua, in 1707, had 1,001 holdings for her 12.9 thousand slaves. By 1712-13, she had 758 white families owning 11.8 thousand blacks. Thus sometime around 1710, Antigua, which now dominates the economy of the Leeward Islands, has on average over thirteen or fourteen slaves per holding. This is a minimum figure because "able men" will exceed "number of holdings."[21]

Moving forward to 1720 figures, the number of slaves on Antigua increased to 19,186 while the count of white free men was down to 739, making the ratio 25:1 (less for holdings). Nevis, St. Christopher, and Montserrat all augmented their slave holdings by 1720, to a total of 16,782.[22] Somewhere between 1707 and 1720, the Leeward Islands moved to a predominantly slave labor force. We can tentatively locate the transition to slavery in the Leeward Islands as sometime around 1710, plus or minus a few years.

This estimate puts the Leeward Islands about fifty years behind Barbados. Modern and contemporary writers make comparable estimates. As Craton points out, the Barbadian slave total for 1680, was not exceeded (in the Leeward Islands) until 1720, and "the rapid increase peaked . . . around 1740 rather than 1690 (for Barbados)."[23] Other estimates of slave imports show a sharp increase in 1724.[24] Writing in 1741 about the Leeward Islands, Oldmixon consigns tobacco, indigo, ginger and other crops to the past or "thirty or forty years ago," and stresses the shift to sugar.[25] Dunn identifies 1713, as the date by which "most of the problems that had stirred the evolution of the Leeward Islands planter class in the 17th century were resolved. . . . Their frontier days were over; they entered into a new era of opulence."[26] If this dating is tentatively accepted for the transition of the Leeward Islands, what factors determine it?

In the 1690s, during the War of the League of Augsburg (1689–97), France rigorously and successfully disputed the supremacy of the seas with England. English trade suffered greatly from French privateering while the English navy was occupied watching the French navy. The high sugar prices of the 1690s reflect the damage to British merchant shipping: marine insurance reached 30 percent. In the War of the Spanish Succession (1702–12), the French navy was practically withdrawn and, though privateers continued to do damage, these years were marked by commercial prosperity in England. This is when sugar of the Leeward Islands becomes important. Postwar prices remain much higher than seventeenth century levels. Barbados remains the dominant sugar supplier until 1710. From 1710 to 1715, she shares top place with the Leeward Islands but after 1715, the Leeward Island exports exceed those of Barbados every year without exception. After 1730, Barbadian exports decline absolutely, never reaching 200,000 cwt. again, and enter a fairly steady decline for the next thirty years.

Thus during the period from 1710 to 1730, the output of the Leeward Islands increases in response to British demand and by supplanting part of the Barbadian output. As Barbados relates to Brazil, so the Leeward Islands relate to Barbados.

English sugar imports remained on a stable trend line through the 1730s and 1740s, and prices began to fall in the 1730s, and did not turn up again until the 1740s. This was the decade of dominance in sugar exports for the Leeward Islands. Her gains come not from English demand increases this time, but from Barbadian decline.

Jamaica was by far the most important sugar colony and last to develop. When the importance of the West Indies was at its height at the end of the eighteenth century, Jamaicans held over a quarter of a million slaves and sent nearly a million hundredweight of sugar to England. But when capital and slaves were pouring into Barbados in the 1650s, it was hard to attract and keep planters in Jamaica, despite generous offers of land from the government. Buccaneering was not only more attractive to many individuals: it was also connived at by the governor in Jamaica and winked at by the government at home. From the occupation in 1655 until 1689, policy toward Jamaica partook of the Elizabethan style of plundering the Spanish.

Planting on Jamaica was slow to develop and sugar monoculture was not a feature. Cacao was the "first principal invitation to the early settlers."[27] Early maps of the island (1671) identifying the crop grown by each planter show sugar dividing the honors with the others on a fifty-fifty basis. Governor Lynch, writing in 1673, identifies cacao, indigo, and hides as important crops. Dunn speaks of Jamaica in 1700 as "a bad joke," the home of a quasi criminal underclass. It is hard to agree with Dunn that "sugar was king" in 1692.

The slow growth of Jamaica until mid-eighteenth century: was a matter of widespread concern in England.[28] When Oldmixon published his second edition in 1741, he tells us that cacao is gone as a principal crop and tobacco is nearly unknown, but indigo and "plenty of cotton and ginger" are grown. "Few islands have so much cattle." In 1741, however, he thinks sugar production had increased tenfold over 1670.[29]

Table 7.2.

Jamaica Year	Sugar Production Thous. Hogsheads 16 cwt.
1722	11
1739	28
1744	35
1768	54
1774	76

Bryan Edwards' estimates in table 7.2 of Jamaican sugar development will give a good picture of what a reliable contemporary observer thought.[30]

Craton locates the beginning of the sugar boom in Jamaica in the 1730s.[31] Not until 1748, does Jamaica sugar production begin to approximate that of the Leeward Islands, not until 1758, does it begin to pull away decisively and enter a period of explosive growth. If a turning point is to be chosen, perhaps Sheridan's "mid-century" is the best choice, again plus or minus several years.

Jamaican growth in the 1730s and 1740s may have been held back by the low prices of those years and by the ability of the Leeward Islands to fill the demand. Prices began rising in the late 1730s, which fits with Craton's timing of the beginning of the boom, but not until 1740 is the price level of 1720 reached. The rise of sugar prices occurs between 1740 and 1760, when they decline a bit and then stabilize at a higher level.

The dynamic factor that is observable from 1750 is the explosive growth of sugar imports. Rapid increase is observed in every decade. This increase is supplied by the take-off of Jamaican sugar production, by the leveling off of production of the Leeward Islands production, and later by the appearance of sugar from the Ceded Islands after the Seven Years' War. The era of the rise of Jamaican sugar is the era of the greatest English slave trade, and it is set off by English sugar demand. A detailed statistical case for this association has been made by David Richardson.[32] The third quarter of the eighteenth century is the preeminent era of sugar and slavery, and Jamaica takes the lead in this era.

English commerce thrived during the Seven Years' War. French privateers captured very large numbers of English merchantmen in the West Indies but, according to a French source "the prodigious growth of the English shipping explains the numbers of these prizes." English naval historians agree "the national prosperity, while waging a long, bloody, and costly war, was never before shown by any people in the world."[33]

The transition to sugar, in the 1650s, in Barbados, in the second decade of the eighteenth century in the Leeward Islands, and in the middle of that century in Jamaica, roughly accords with the pattern of slave imports. The slave trade of the seventeenth century illustrates Brazilian dominance and the rise of Barbados. According to Curtin,[34] Brazil received 42 percent of the Atlantic slave trade in that century, the Caribbean 32 percent—of which latter the British islands accounted for nineteen percent. Barbados was by far the largest British importer. Before 1676, only Barbados had any considerable number of slaves at all (seventy thousand), while the Leeward Islands had twelve thousand and Jamaica only eight thousand.

Jamaican imports overtook Barbados in the final quarter of the century with the Leeward Islands still lagging behind. Not only is the absolute size of Jamaica so much greater than the other islands, she always had a blacker population profile than they. She was settled later and never experienced the thick population of small holders in the tobacco era characteristic of some the others.

In the eighteenth century Curtin's data show Barbadian slave imports declining every period from 1701–20.[35] The Leeward Islands imports rise to a peak in 1741–60, and level off in the subsequent twenty years. Jamaican imports, however, rise in every period through the entire century, and had not yet reached their peak until the nineteenth century. A complete correlation of slave imports with transition to sugar cannot really be expected, since imports will also reflect demographic developments in the West Indies and the changing labor needs of planters as productivity per unit of output declines. Nevertheless, it is clear that the time pattern of the slave trade is more closely tied to the transition to sugar than to the relative price of slaves and indentures.

Summary and Conclusions

This paper addresses the transition to slavery as an industrial system in the British West Indies.

The explanations for the appearance of modern slavery are of three kinds. Classical economists like Merivale and Cairnes associated slavery with free land. Neoclassical economists have a conceptual scheme of great generality, and the emphasis in particular historical cases has been on the relative prices of slave and indentured labor. Traditional historians have associated the introduction of slavery in the modern era with sugar production, but have provided no economic framework to account for the phenomenon. These approaches encounter serious problems in explaining events in the British West Indies.

The present paper argues that the profitability of free and slave labor varies substantially between crops and that the demand for slaves is in part derived from the demand for the commodities where slaves have productivity advantages. Authors who concentrate on the relative cost of free and slave labor, and view the choice of crop as an exogenous variable, outside the system, will miss the most important factors in explaining the course of slavery in the British West Indies.

Demand conditions in England and cost conditions in the islands explain the timing of transition to slavery in the British West Indies: in Barbados in the 1650s, in the Leeward Islands around 1710, in Jamaica around the middle of the eighteenth century. Data on the quantity and direction of slave imports correspond roughly with this dating. The largest trade in slaves and sugar occurred in the third quarter of the eighteenth century Jamaica was the principal island economy at this time, and shifts in England motivated the development.

The elastic supply of especially productive slave labor is necessary for the development of slavery in an industrial system, but is not a sufficient explanation for the introduction of slavery into particular places at particular times. For this we need to look at charts 7.1, 7.2 and 7.3 as they illustrate factors that govern the demand for those commodities in which slavery has special advantages.

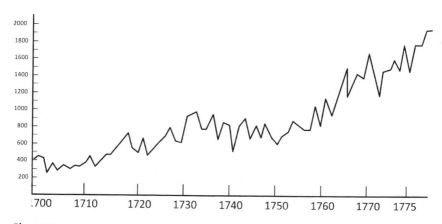

Chart 7.1.

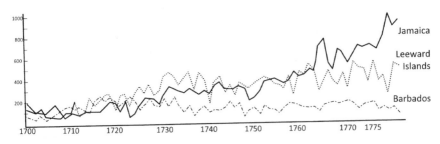

Chart 7.2.

Chart 7.3.

Notes

1. John Hicks, A *Theory of Economic History*, (Oxford, 1969), 131.

2. Adam Smith, *Wealth of Nations*, ed. Edwin Cannon, (New York, Modern Library), 365.

3. Herman Merivale, *Lectures on Colonisation and Colonies*, reprinted, (Oxford, 1928). Merivale is only one classical economist with this approach. Cairnes and Wakefield are among the others.

4. Barbara L. Solow, "Capitalism and Slavery in the Exceedingly Long Run," unpublished paper delivered at a Conference on Caribbean Salvery and British Capitalism held at Bellagio, May 22–25, 1984. David Galenson, *White Servitude in Colonial America: an Economic Analysis*, (Cambridge, Mass., 1981), 126. See also Henry A. Gemery and Jan S. Hogendorn, "Atlantic Slave Trade: A Tentative Economic Model," *Journal of African History*, XV, 1974, 223: "Relative labour price patters dictated a choice of slave labour on plantations when initial shifts to labor-intensive staple crops took place."

5. Richard N. Bean and Robert P. Thomas, "The Adoption of Slavery in British America," in Henry A. Gemery and Jan S. Hogendorn eds., *The Uncommon Market: Essays in the Economic History of the Atlantic Slave Trade*, (New York, 1979).

6. Gemery and Hogendorn, *op. cit.*

7. Russel Menard, "From Servants to Slaves: The Transformation of the Chesapeake Labor System," *Southern Studies*, XVI, 1977, 355–390.

8. Outstanding examples are Carl and Roberta Bridenbaugh, *No Peace Beyond the Line: the English in the Caribbean 1624–1690*, (New York, 1972); Richard S. Dunn, *Sugar and Slaves: the Rise of the Planter Class in the English West Indies 1624–1713*. (Chapel Hill, NC, 1972); Richard B. Sheridan; *Sugar and Slavery: an Economic History of the British West Indies 1623–1775*, (Baltimore, Maryland, 1973).

9. Ralph Gray and Betty Wood, "Transition from Indentured Servant to Involuntary Servitude in Colonial Georgia," *Explorations in Economic History*, XIII, 1976

10. The literature on rising costs in sugar production is large and goes back a long way. Francis Bacon observed that "being the first in an invention does sometimes cause a wonderful overgrowth of riches, as it was with the first sugarmen in the Canaries." When sugar is planted in virgin: soil, crop can be harvested for years (from side shoots) without replanting. Subsequently, canes must be replanted regularly. Applications of fertilizer must be undertaken to maintain soil quality after the soil loses its original nutrients, and fertilization increases weeds. The supply of fuel for sugar mills also involves increasing costs.

11. Gloria L. Main, *Tobacco Colony: Life in Early Maryland 1650–1720*, (Princeton, 1982), ch. 3. This does not imply a complete absence of racism. The quotation continues "but close reading of the evidence reveals that racial boundaries did exist and were carefully observed."

12. Paul G.E. Clemens, *The Atlantic Economy and Colonial Maryland's Eastern Shore: From Tobacco to Grain*, (Ithaca, NY, 1980); and Allan Kulikoff, "Origins of Afro-American Society in Tidewater Maryland and Virginia, 1700 to 1790," *William and Mary Quarterly*, XXXV, 1978.

13. Peter H. Wood, "More Like A Negro Country," Demographic Patterns in Colonial South Carolina, 1700–1740," in Stanley L. Engerman and Eugene D. Genovese, eds., *Race and Slavery in the Western Hemisphere: Quantitative Studies*, (Princeton, 1975). A wealthy rice parish could have a 3:1 slave ratio.

14. *Cf. Groans of the Plantation or a True Account of their Grievous and Extreme Sufferings by the Heavy Impositions Upon Sugar, and Other Hardships, Relating more particularly to the Island of Barbados*, London, 1689. Forty Barbadian sugar estates were abandoned by 1689. Fuel and fertilizer costs had increased, and according to Deer, coal was actually imported from Newcastle, Noel Deer, *History of Sugar*, 2 vols., (London, 1949–50), vol. I 64.

15. Fernand Braudel, *The Structures of Everyday Life: the Limites of the Possible*, trans. Sian Reynolds, New York, 1981, p. 225.

16. Matthew Edel, "The Brazilian Sugar Cycle of the Seventeenth Century and the Rise of West Indian Competition," *Caribbean Studies*, IX, 1969. Without agreeing with his conclusions, I would like to acknowledge the helpfulness of this article.

17. I would like to acknowledge the useful work by Robert Carlisle Batie, "A comparative Economic History of the Spanish, French, and English on the Caribbean Islands during the Seventeenth Century," Ph. D. Dissertation, University of Washington, 1972 and "Why Sugar? Economic Cycles and the Changing Staples in the English and French Antilles 1624-54." Price data on sugar, indigo, and tobacco

come from N.W. Posthumas, An Inquiry into the History of Prices in Holland, (Leiden, 1946), reproduced in Batie, 4, 6, 29, 30.

18. Dunn, op. cit., p. 117.

19. Quoted in Vere Langford Oliver, History of the Island of Antigua, one of the Leeward Caribbees in the West Indies, from the first settlement in 1635 to the Present Time, 3 vols., (London, 1894), vol. I, ch. 5.

20. Quoted in C.S.S. Hingham, The Development of the Leeward Islands Under the Restorations 1660-1688: A Study of the Foundations of the Old Colonial System, (Cambridge, England), 1921, 187–88. In 1672 (ibid.), Col. Warner wrote of St. Christopher "no person will venture upon it because there can be no prospect of gaming or making an estate but spending one."

21. Reprinted in Oliver, op. cit., ch. 6.

22. Idem.

23. Michael Craton, Sinews of Empire. A Short History of British Slavery, (Anchor Books edition, New York, 1974), 45; Craton sees the same patterns in the Leeward Islands as in Barbados, with a fifty-year lag.

24. Oliver, op. cit., ch. 6. The figures are 1720, 251; 1721, 449; 1722, 584; 1723, 430; but then 1724, 1,525; 1725, 1,645; 1726, 2,183; 1727, 1,365; and 1728, 2,846.

25. John Oldmixon, British Empire in America, 2 vols., 2nd ed. 1741 (reprinted New York, 1969), vol. II, 197, 230, 232.

26. Dunn, op. cit., 148.

27. Oldmixon, op. cit., vol. II, 396. Gov. Lynch is quoted in Oliver, op. cit., ch. 5; Dunn, op. cit., 149.

28. Sheridan, op. cit., 216. Cf ibid., 222: "Just as the low state of the sugar market had been the most pervasive factor in Jamaica's slow growth and internal dissension down to 1740, so it was that the subsequent expansion of the economy came in response to a rising market."

29. Oldmixon, op. cit., vol. 1, 406, 413.

30. Bryan Edwards, The History Civil and Commercial of the British Colonies in the West Indies, 3rd ed., 3 vols., (London, 1801), 301–302. His figure #rir 1739 has been converted from 14 lb. M. to 16 lb. M.

31. Craton, op. cit., p. 46: "The Jamaican sugar boom began in earnest in the 1730s."

32. David Richardson, "Slave Trade, Sugar, and British Economic Growth 1748 to 1776," unpublished paper presented at a Conference on Caribbean Slavery and British Capitalism held at Bellagio, May 22–25, 1984.

33. Quoted in Alfred Thayer Mahan, The Influence as Sea Power upon History 1500–1783, reprinted, (Sagamare Press, New York, 1957), 118. Mahan attributes this to errors in French strategy in pursuing a policy of cruising Warfare. He contrasts it with French strategy in the American Revolutionary Wars.

34. Philip D. Curtin, The Atlantic Slave Trade: A Census, (Madison, Wisconsin, 1969), Table 34, 119.

35. Curtin, op. cit., Table 40, 141.

~

Publication History

"Capitalism and Slavery in the Exceedingly Long Run." Originally published in *British Capitalism & Caribbean Slavery: The Legacy of Eric Williams*, ed. Barbara L. Solow & Stanley L. Engerman, Cambridge University Press 1987, paperback 2004, pp 51–77. Reprinted with permission of Cambridge University Press.

"Slavery and Colonization" Originally published in *Slavery and the Rise of the Atlantic System*, ed. Barbara L. Solow, Cambridge University Press 1991, paperback 1993, pp 21–42. Reprinted with permission of Cambridge University Press.

"Why Columbus Failed: The New World Without Slavery." Originally published in *Nord und Süd in Amerika*, ed. Wolfgang Reinhard & Peter Waldmann, *Rombach Verlag*, 1992, pp 1111–1124. Reprinted with permission of *Rombach Verlag*.

"Caribbean Slavery and British Growth: The Eric Williams Hypothesis." Originally published in *Journal of Development Economics*, Vol. 17 (1985) pp 99–115. Reprinted with permission of *Journal of Development Economics*.

"The Transition to Plantation Slavery: The Case of the British West Indies." Originally published in *Actes du Colloque International sur la traite des Noirs*,

Centre de Recherche sur l'Histoire du Monde Atlantique, Société Française d'Histoire d'Outre-Mer, Nantes 1985, pp 89–110. Reprinted with permission of Centre de Recherche sur l'Histoire du Monde Atlantique, Société Française d'Histoire d'Outre-Mer.

Index

Brenner, Robert, 100–101, 109n3
Bridenbaughs, 115
Britain: Atlantic trading system
causing economic changes in, 51,
107; British American colonies
tobacco investments of, 94n11;
British American colonies with
goods from, 33–34; British West
Indies economic value to, 32, 80;
Caribbean slavery and growth of,
20; colonial demand for exports
of, 91; early industrialization of,
90–91; export growth of, 19; as first
industrial nation, 56; investment's
rate of return of, 21; national
income and slavery profits of,
83–88, 84, 91; Portuguese-Brazilian
economy and, 23n27; rates of
return of, 94n9; slavery creating
Industrial Revolution in, xiii–xiv,
48, 77; slavery of, 20, 21; slave/sugar
complex influence on, 16, 51–52;
slave trade influencing, 48; sugar
imports of, 16, 31; sugar prices rising
and, 120; United States and export
growth of, 20–21; William and
Mary's accession to throne of, 50–51;
Williams and economic growth of,
94n6
British American colonies: agriculture
in, 71–72; Atlantic trading system
ties to, 43; black and white
population growth of, 31; black
slaves used in, 26; British West
Indies impacted by, 54–55; colonial
products traded with, 25; commodity
exports of slave colonies in, 32;
English manufactured goods in,
33–34; European markets and
shipping rates of, 55; free white
person wealth in, 33; immigrants
recreating what they left behind
in, 42; natural resources of, 73;

population and economic growth
in, 17, 40–41; slavery in, 30–31,
31, 32, 34–35, 57, 107; slaves and
population growth of, 17, 30–31,
31, 40–41; timber abundant in, 29;
tobacco investments in, 94n11;
white and black Diaspora flowing to,
41. See also colonies
British West Indies, 90; Britain's
economic value of, 32, 80; British
American colonies impact on,
54–55; high rate of return from, 81;
labor types for, 116–17; landlord
savings in, 95n13; plantation slavery
in, 115–16; pre-slave era of, 70–71;
slavery era of, xv, 74, 114, 126–27;
Spain's incursion in to, 63–65
bullion imports, 66, 68

cacao, 124
Cain, P. J., 20–21
Cairnes, 126
Canary Islands, 8–10
Cape Verde islands, 11
capital, investments and profits, 89, 90,
98
capital asset, 4–5, 86
capitalism, 98–99, 101–3
Capitalism and Slavery (Williams), xiv,
47, 54, 79–80, 86, 90
capitalist development, 21n1, 99
capitalist principles, xiv
Caribbean Islands, 14, 16, 20, 70, 81
Carr, 34
central tendencies model, 39
Chaunu, Pierre, 7, 10, 66
Child, Josiah, 86
Chile-Peru-Charcas, 68
Civil War, 58
Clark, G. Kitson, 56
class formation, 100
classical economists, 112, 126
Cobb-Douglas model, 77, 88, 92

~

About the Author

Barbara L. Solow graduated from Radcliffe College in 1945, and earned an MA and PhD from Harvard University. She has served as Associate Professor of Economics at Boston University and then as Research Associate at the W.E.B. DuBois Institute of African-American Studies at Harvard. Her research interests and extensive writings have centered on two large topics: Irish nineteenth century economic history and the causes and consequences of plantation slavery in the British West Indies. She is co-editor (with Colin Palmer) of a forthcoming conference volume honoring Eric Williams as scholar and statesman, and she is currently completing a book on Anthony Trollope and Ireland: The Novelist as Eyewitness.